About the Tech Editors

W9-AVT-210

Angie Jones is currently an animator at Sony Pictures Imageworks (SPI) producing animation for the characters in *Stuart Little 2*, to be released April 2002. Previous to SPI, Angie worked as a Lead Artist at Angel Studios. She has also worked as a character animator for Oddworld Inhabitants on the award-winning Abe's Exoddus. From 1995 through 1998, Angie worked on over 25 character-driven educational software products for the Playstation at The Lightspan Partnership, Inc. Angie has also worked as a 2D/3D animator for the children's educational television show *Reality Check*, among others during her freelance career in Atlanta, Georgia. She is also the coauthor of the books *Inside 3D Studio Max 2, Volume III: Animation* (New Riders, 1998) and *3D Studio Max 3 Professional Animation* (New Riders, 2000). For additional information about Angie Jones, go to http://www.spicycricket.com.

Sean Miller, who has a background in fine arts, theater, and computer graphics, is a character animator at Oddworld Inhabitants. The head of the real-time animation team for the 3D adventure game Oddworld: Munch's Oddysee, he has also worked on the in-game character animations and the award-winning cinematics for the game Oddworld: Abe's Exoddus.

Trademarks

All terms mentioned in this book that are known to be trademarks or service marks have been appropriately capitalized. New Riders Publishing cannot attest to the accuracy of this information. Use of a term in this book should not be regarded as affecting the validity of any trademark or service mark.

Warning and Disclaimer

Every effort has been made to make this book as complete and as accurate as possible, but no warranty of fitness is implied. The information provided is on an "as is" basis. The authors and the publisher shall have neither liability nor responsibility to any person or entity with respect to any loss or damages arising from the information contained in this book.

digital
character
animation 2,
volume II:
advanced
techniques

george maestri

New Riders

201 West 103rd Street, Indianapolis, Indiana, 46290

Publisher
David Dwyer

Associate Publisher
Al Valvano

Executive Editor
Steve Weiss

Product Marketing Manager
Kathy Malmloff

Publicist
Susan Nixon

Managing Editor
Sarah Kearns

Acquisitions Editor
Leah Williams

Development Editor
Jennifer Eberhardt

Project Editor
Linda Seifert

Copy Editor
Margo Catts

Technical Editors
Angie Jones
Sean Miller

Cover Artwork
George Maestri

Cover Designer
Aren Howell

Interior Designer
Sandra Schroeder

Compositor
Kim Scott

Proofreader
Jeannie Smith

Indexer
Lisa Stumpf

Digital Character Animation 2, Volume II: Advanced Techniques

Copyright © 2002 by New Riders Publishing

International Standard Book Number: 0-7357-0044-3

Library of Congress Catalog Card Number: 00-101495

Printed in the United States of America

First Printing: August 2001

06   05   04   03   02   7   6   5   4   3   2   1

Interpretation of the printing code: The rightmost double-digit number is the year of the book's printing; the rightmost single-digit number is the number of the book's printing. For example, the printing code 02-1 shows that the first printing of the book occurred in 2002.

About the Author

Growing up in Arizona, **George Maestri** was well renowned as the kid who could always draw a really cool Camaro. He got his first taste of computers before high school when he taught himself to program computer games on his Dad's mainframe. He landed his first programming job at age 16, writing code for the Altair 8800. He earned a degree in computer science and Silicon Valley quickly seduced him, where he worked as an engineer on early Unix-based graphics systems in the '80s. After a few years, he noticed that the people who created art on computers had a lot more fun than the engineers who made the machines. This sparked an early midlife crisis and George embarked on a career change.

George enrolled in the animation program at DeAnza College in Cupertino, California, and was soon making his own student films. There he met Joe Murray, who had just pitched an animated series idea to Nickelodeon. Joe hired George to help with development of *Rocko's Modern Life*. Soon after that, George found himself working day and night on the pilot as an animator and assistant producer. Miraculously, the show was picked up, and George moved to Los Angeles in 1993, where he worked on *Rocko's Modern Life* as a writer for the entire run of the show, earning a Cable Ace nomination in the process.

During his time at Nickelodeon, George taught himself 3D animation. His interest in this subject soon landed him a monthly column covering 3D animation for *DV* magazine. George has continued working as a freelance journalist, writing articles on animation production for magazines such as *Computer Graphics World*, *Animation Magazine*, *Film & Video*, and *Digital Magic*.

In 1995, George found himself at Film Roman as a writer and creator, developing new concepts for animated series. Several of his projects were picked up for development by major networks. George also got his first taste of 3D animation production, animating a 3D Felix for the CBS Series *The Twisted Tales of Felix the Cat*.

George worked as a freelance animation director until he was hired as the original animation producer on *South Park* in 1997. In this capacity, George ramped up production and hired the original staff of artists, animators, and technical directors. He also used his computer background to develop the techniques and technology for animating cut-out characters using Alias.

After *South Park*, George went back to freelancing and found himself on the road. He taught animation at NanYang Polytechnic in Singapore and then flew to Paris to direct a live-action/3D pilot at Medialab for Film Roman. George then became an animation consultant at Curious Pictures in New York, where he helped set up the production of *A Little Curious*, the first TV series animated in Maya.

During this time, George was creating and pitching his own projects. He sold two properties into development: *The Experts* (co-developed with Jerry Beck) to Warner Bros., and *The Forgotten Ones* to Disney/ABC. George wrote and directed both pilots.

In 1999, *The Experts* was renamed *Karen & Kirby* and George's characters became part of the Kids WB family. George set up the production and directed all 13 of the three-minute episodes, which aired during *The Big Cartoonie Show*. George, along with Jerry Beck, also acted as story editor. One of these episodes, "When Animals Go Berserk," was shown to wide acclaim at a number of festivals, including the LA Animation Celebration and Siggraph 2000.

George is the author of *Digital Character Animation 2, Volume I: Essential Techniques* (New Riders, 1999). He is also the editor of the New Riders [digital] series.

Dedication

This book is dedicated to my kids.

Acknowledgments

I'd like to thank all of the people at New Riders for their extreme patience and wonderful support; my family for their support and all the software vendors—Discreet, Alias|Wavefront, Softimage, and many others for allowing me the chance to use their tools. Thanks also to Jerry Beck, Warren Fuller, Sean Miller, Jackie Watson, John Baurley, Carlos Juliao, Warner Bros., and everyone else who worked on *Karen & Kirby*: Angie Jones, Annette Van Duren, Laura Lawson, Renee Hatcher, and finally, all the animators who've helped me and given me advice over the years.

A Message from New Riders

As the reader of this book, you are our most important critic and commentator. We value your opinion and want to know what we're doing right, what we could do better, in what areas you'd like to see us publish, and any other words of wisdom you're willing to pass our way.

As Executive Editor at New Riders, I welcome your comments. You can fax, email, or write me directly to let me know what you did or didn't like about this book—as well as what we can do to make our books better. When you write, please be sure to include this book's title, ISBN, and author, as well as your name and phone or fax number. I will carefully review your comments and share them with the authors and editors who worked on the book.

Please note that I cannot help you with technical problems related to the topic of this book, and that due to the high volume of email I receive, I might not be able to reply to every message. Thanks.

Email: steve.weiss@newriders.com

Mail: Steve Weiss
            Executive Editor
            New Riders Publishing
            201 West 103rd Street
            Indianapolis, IN 46290 USA

Visit Our Web Site: www.newriders.com

On our Web site, you'll find information about our other books, the authors we partner with, book updates and file downloads, promotions, discussion boards for online interaction with other users and with technology experts, and a calendar of trade shows and other professional events with which we'll be involved. We hope to see you around.

Email Us from Our Web Site

Go to www.newriders.com and click on the Contact Us link if you

- Have comments or questions about this book.
- Want to report errors that you have found in this book.
- Have a book proposal or are interested in writing for New Riders.
- Would like us to send you one of our author kits.
- Are an expert in a computer topic or technology and are interested in being a reviewer or technical editor.

- Want to find a distributor for our titles in your area.

- Are an educator/instructor who wants to preview New Riders books for classroom use. In the body/comments area, include your name, school, department, address, phone number, office days/hours, text currently in use, and enrollment in your department, along with your request for either desk/examination copies or additional information.

Call Us or Fax Us

You can reach us toll-free at (800) 571-5840 + 0 (ask for New Riders). If outside the U.S., please call 1-317-581-3500 and ask for New Riders. If you prefer, you can fax us at 1-317-581-4663, Attention: New Riders.

Technical Support for This Book   Although we encourage entry-level users to get as much as they can out of our books, keep in mind that our books are written assuming a non-beginner level of user-knowledge of the technology. This assumption is reflected in the brevity and shorthand nature of some of the tutorials.

New Riders will continually work to create clearly written, thoroughly tested and reviewed technology books of the highest educational caliber and creative design. We value our customers more than anything—that's why we're in this business—but we cannot guarantee to each of the thousands of you who buy and use our books that we will be able to work individually with you through tutorials or content with which you may have questions. We urge readers who need help in working through exercises or other material in our books—and who need this assistance immediately—to use as many of the resources that our technology and technical communities can provide, especially the many online user groups and list servers available.

Contents at a Glance

Table of Contents

Introduction

When we decided to break up the original *Digital Character Animation* into two volumes, I had no idea how long this second volume would take to write. I apologize to those who were expecting this book sooner. Production can be a very demanding job, and squeezing a book into my schedule took a lot more time that I'd imagined. To add a bit of irony to the equation, production is exactly what this book is about.

Animation is basically a series of tricks. The goal is to trick the audience into believing a screen full of flickering pixels is actually alive. In the last book, you learned the basic tricks, or language of animation, by learning squash and stretch, anticipation, and so on. This book takes the basics a step further to show you how to animate in the real world—to make your own film, or work on somebody else's film, as well as how to really think like an animator.

When I initially planned this book, I thought we'd include chapters on advanced modeling, textures, lighting, and so on. As I got deeper into these subjects, we realized that each of these topics deserved its own book. The first book, *Digital Lighting & Rendering*, was written by Jeremy Birn, and we've added Owen Demer's *Digital Texturing & Painting* to the series as well. We're also planning more books that go into depth on a number of other computer graphics and special effects-related topics.

What You Should Know

Before you begin this book, you should have a fundamental understanding of computers, computer graphics, and 3D software. This book will not bore you with a dissertation on CPUs, RAM, and hard disks, nor will it bother you by explaining such things as pixels, alpha channels, and rendering. If you don't know these terms, then you need to study the fundamentals of computer graphics. You should also be familiar with your chosen 3D software. Work through your software's manuals and tutorials to understand its features.

What You Will Need

All you need to animate characters digitally is a computer and a 3D package. An extremely basic package handles only simple characters, however, and some packages lend themselves to character animation more readily than others. Look for packages that support features such as shape animation, skeletal deformation, multiple target morphing, and inverse kinematics, among others.

Beginning animators should decide on the software they want to use before buying any hardware. Each hardware platform has its selling points, but it's the software that you use to animate your characters. When buying hardware, always try to buy the fastest machine with the most memory. Systems become obsolete quickly, so an investment in a fast machine lasts much longer than an investment in a slower one. Of course, if you're broke, it is still entirely possible to produce terrific animation on almost any budget, and used equipment can be the basement animator's secret weapon. Quality is not a function of processor speed.

The real lure of digital animation is interactivity, or the ability it gives you to play back your animations on-the-fly and make changes immediately. The faster your machine is, the higher the level of interactivity and the smoother the flow of the creative process. To help speed things along, a 3D accelerator card helps you play back shaded animation tests interactively as you create. Not all 3D cards are created equal, so check with your software vendor for a list of supported 3D cards before you buy.

Another important issue is output. Almost any computer can play back thumbnail-sized animations directly on your computer screen. For your own tests, this type of playback is perfectly acceptable. If you want to print to videotape, however, you need to include a full-motion video card for final output. These cards come in many flavors: some output only analog video, some only digital video, some both. Your choice of card depends on your choice for final output—if you own only a VHS deck, then analog will have to do. After your creations are printed to tape, anybody can view them.

About This Book's Approach to Software

It would have been much easier to write this book using specific software packages. But a tutorial using Brand X software would prove somewhat useless to the person using Brand Y software, not to mention those who work in studios that use proprietary software. And as soon as Brand X got a slew of new features or a new interface, this book would be headed for the trash. Besides, you already own a book about the software—it's called the manual.

This book takes on a bigger challenge—to serve as a guide for anyone with a computer and a 3D package. The principles presented here are done from a package-neutral standpoint. It is my hope that this book will be applicable over a broad range of platforms. Therefore, the book focuses on the many features of these packages that are similar.

The more you work with different 3D packages, the more you will realize how similar they really are to each other. Polygonal modeling in one package is very similar to polygonal modeling in another. Some of the terminology may be a bit different between packages, but the underlying geometry and placement of detail on the model are identical.

This book does have to jump through a few hoops when it comes to terminology. The exact same feature in one package may be called something completely different in another package. Where a conflict exists, I have tried to choose the term most commonly used among all packages.

A Final Note

Animating characters is a life-long journey, and this book will help you take only the first few steps. Animation can be incredibly fun, but it's also a very difficult art to master. After finishing this book, it will take many years of practice to become a true animator. I hope you will rely on this reference throughout your journey.

CHAPTER 1

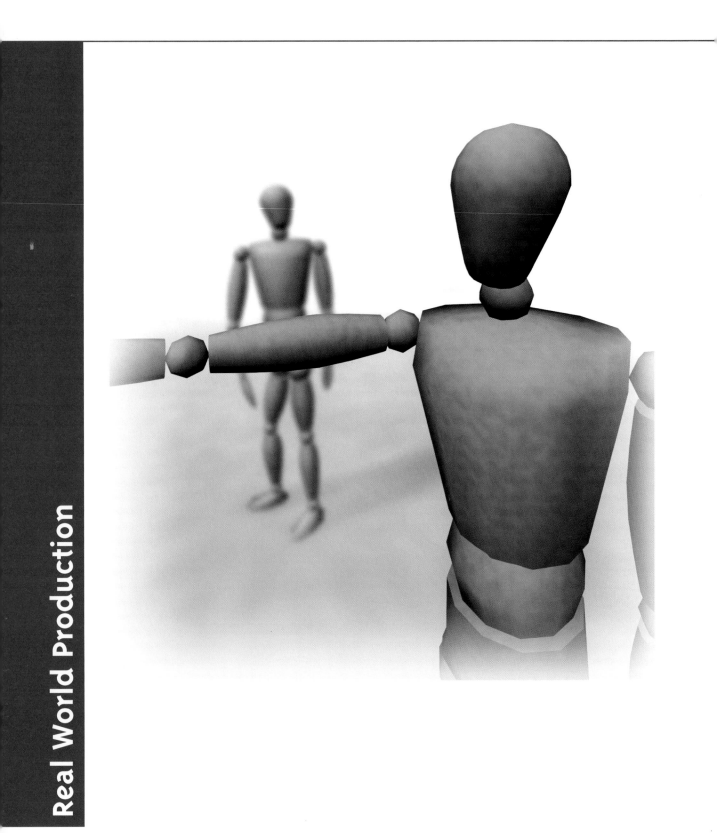

Real World Production

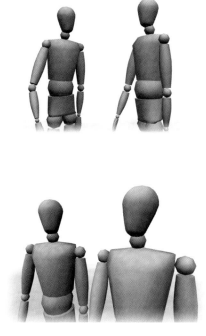

D*igital Character Animation 2, Volume I* taught you the basics of animation. This second volume is about the next step—how to turn that animation into a film, video, game, or whatever the next format may be. Understanding the basics of production will help you focus your efforts, or the efforts of your team, to get the most out of a film.

The great thing about animation is that it can be a solitary pursuit. A good animator with a good idea can make a very entertaining film. Contrast that to live-action films, where multiple people are required—actors, camera operators, sound technicians, and so on. Making a film all by yourself can be excellent training in every aspect of filmmaking.

Of course, those in a commercial setting will most likely be working on some sort of team, which may include producers, directors, animators, and writers, among others. Knowing how all the bits and pieces fit together is certain to help you, regardless of the particular job you have.

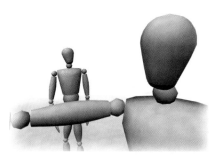

Getting Started in Filmmaking

Making an animated film is not an easy task. You need to be organized and dedicated to completing it. Whether making a student film or a feature, the steps required to make and finish an animated film are pretty much the same.

The process starts with the producers assembling a team. Writers and storyboard artists create a story, while other artists are developing the look of the production and setting up characters. When the story is locked, the dialogue is recorded and the animation blocked out. Finally, the animators work their magic, while other artists create special effects and render the frames. The project is then delivered on film, video, the Internet, or some other medium.

People

Regardless of the number of actual people involved, there are quite a few job descriptions associated with filmmaking, and you'll need to be familiar with each of them. If you're working alone, you may find that you'll be doing most or all of these jobs yourself. If, however, you're working as part of a larger team, you may be doing only one of these jobs, or in the case of smaller productions, you may find that you're managing a handful of tasks. Regardless of where you find yourself, the following list highlights the job descriptions.

Producers. These come in a number of flavors. At the top of the heap is the executive producer, who does the business development and funds the project. The executive producers typically are the ones who deal with clients. A bit lower on the totem pole may be a supervising producer, who manages the day-to-day tasks and might delegate responsibility to even more producers. These might include line producers, creative producers, animation producers, and perhaps a few others. Generally, all producers are involved in managing the production in one way or another.

Director. The main creative force on the project. The director supervises just about everything, including story, dialogue recording, modeling, animation, and post-production.

Writer/Storyboard. The people who create and visualize the story. Writers tend to work with words; storyboard artists tend to work with pictures. Both have the same goal of coming up with clever pictures and a coherent story.

Note

Some studios break up the directing job. They may have a voice director, who does nothing but direct the voice talent, an animation director, art director, creative director, and so on.

Voice Talent. The voices of the characters. A good voice actor has a very nimble and versatile voice and excellent acting skills.

Modeling. A sculptor, essentially, who works on a computer and creates all the characters and props. Some modelers who have been known to dabble in clay may scan in their physical sculptures. A good modeler knows how to build characters that animate well.

Textures/Lighting. A painter who works on the computer. The texture artist is responsible for creating textures and writing shaders that are applied to the characters and props. Many times, the texture person also manages lighting, though this is not always the case.

Technical Director. An artist with a strong technical bent. Technical directors know a lot about the software and can usually do some programming. They do all sorts of tasks, from rigging characters to laying out scenes, doing camera work, writing shaders, and managing renders to writing custom software and plug-ins.

Animator. The person who brings the characters to life. A good animator has an excellent sense of acting and timing, as well as strong knowledge of anatomy and motion.

Systems and Support. The people who keep the computers running. This team can also include people dubbed "render wranglers," who manage rendering and final output on large projects, making sure each and every frame finds its way through the system.

Audio. People who record dialogue, as well as edit and mix the final soundtrack.

Composer. If there is music, someone has to write it—that's the composer. A good composer writes music that sets a mood but doesn't overpower the film.

Administrative. Of course, there are plenty of spots for administrative people—production assistants, payroll, and so on.

> **Note**
>
> Many modelers, like production designers, lean toward either the organic character modeling or the industrial architectural style of modeling. If you can find an artist who can develop both facets, you've struck gold.

Getting Money

Making a film usually involves money, and there are a number of ways to fund a film. If it's a personal or student film, then it's usually funded out of your own pocket or through Aunt Visa and Uncle MasterCard. Some people manage to get grants from nonprofit organizations. In a professional environment, studios request bids and proposals as they do in most businesses. Getting the bid through relies on business contacts, a history of quality work done on time and budget, as well as other factors. More often than not, getting the job also requires that you submit the lowest bid, which makes efficient production a necessity.

Of course, whenever you receive money for work, you give up a certain degree of control. Typically, the person who's writing the checks has the final say. For those who don't want to give up control, the only route is to finance and produce the project yourself.

Pitching Ideas

If you have an idea for something such as a TV series or a feature film, then you might want to start your search for money by pitching the idea to a studio or network. This usually requires putting your concept on paper, creating character designs, writing a sample script, and so on. A lot of animators have taken to creating a short demo film of their concept, which can be played for the executives. It's always best to show people your concept rather than try to explain it in words. Remember, the demo film is just a sales tool—keep it brief and to the point. It's much better to whet the appetite of the executives with a short film than to bore them with a long one.

Creating a short demo film of your characters is a good way to sell your concept.

Getting your foot in the door to get the pitch meeting in the first place is another issue altogether. Probably the best way to do this is to go work in the business and make contacts. A good reputation among the studios helps immensely when you're trying to sell your own ideas.

Another route is to get someone to represent you, such as an agent. The agent takes a cut of the proceeds but should be able to open a few doors for you.

Development Deals

With a great pitch and a bit of luck, you might actually sell your idea into development. A development deal, sometimes called an *option*, usually gives the studio ownership of the idea for a set length of time— anywhere from a few months to a few years. In return for this, they give you some money and help you "develop" the concept. This can mean that the studio pays you to create stories and scripts and perhaps animate a pilot. The studio can also develop the concept by hiring someone else to write the script, which can be a bit shocking to the novice.

If you do get a development deal, then you'll certainly need to get someone on your side to help you. Good agents are pretty skilled in negotiating, as are good entertainment lawyers. Even with help, however, your position in the negotiation depends on your skill and experience. If you haven't sold anything before, you may have to give up quite a bit. The bottom line is that the studio almost always ends up owning the property. As the creator, you get royalties and perhaps a portion of the merchandising rights, as well as creative input into the production of the project. By selling it, however, you do give up ultimate control of your creation. Sometimes, if an idea is good, a studio or network might option your property just to keep it out of the hands of rival networks. Your project then languishes in development hell for a year or two. Avoiding this is tough, but a good agent or lawyer should try to set goals and deadlines in the contract to keep the process moving.

Budgets

So, now you have a little bit of money to produce your film, or just a free summer, a computer, and a heck of a lot of time. In either event, you need to develop a rough budget. With any project, there are three conflicting goals:

> Make the best quality film…
> at the lowest possible price…
> as quickly as possible.

When confronted with these choices, the typical response is to pick two. The trick is to balance all three so you get a film that works but also comes in on time and budget. Doing so may require clever design, scheduling, budgeting, or freebies from a friend at the post house. However you get it done, try to make quality your number one goal, because when people see a film they judge it by quality, not by how much it cost or how quickly it was produced.

There are plenty of good examples of quality films produced for little money. One stellar example is *405, the movie*. Bruce Branit and Jeremy Hunt created the film in only three months, with the only expense being their time and personal home computers. The short film is about a DC-10 that lands on an urban freeway and is feature-quality.

Sadly, nobody has infinite resources, and all animated films have a budget. Animation is a very creative pursuit, and placing time and limits on the creative process is never easy. That's why they invented things like producers to do the dirty work of creating a budget. A budget can be monetary, but it can also take other forms. Deadlines and airdates must be considered, as well as the number of people available to work on the project.

A budget is simply a limit—of time, money, or quality. If you had an infinite amount of time to get something done, chances are good that it would never get done. Limits are good in that they force you to make decisions, invent novel solutions, and—most importantly—get the project finished.

Deadlines

Time, or rather the lack of it, is always a factor when making a film. Part of a budget is the time allotted to complete the project. Most commercial projects have very strict deadlines, and even student films are due at the end of the semester. The only project that might have no deadlines is the personal film. Without a deadline, however, many personal films tend to sit around for years before they get finished. Deadlines are good in that, like budgets, they force you to make decisions that make the project move along. It's best to think of a deadline as the finish line of a race. Finishing the race gives you a sense of accomplishment.

A good budget has reasonable deadlines. As is often the case when money is involved, however, many budgets tend to cut corners. Shaving a week or a month off the schedule may save production money, but it is sure to also dig into the quality of the finished project.

How Much Time?

Deciding exactly how much time to budget a project requires years of experience. Most novices (and many experts, for that matter) tend to underestimate the amount of time required. It almost always takes longer than you think. If in doubt, always add a fudge factor—double or triple your original estimate.

You can use many rules of thumb when budgeting a project. One may be the number of seconds an animator can produce in a week. Of course, this number may vary widely depending on the project. An animator on a feature film may produce only 3–10 seconds per week, but it is very high-quality animation. Games are another story. For the short cinematic sequences in games, 3–10 seconds a day, and for gameplay at least three moves a day. An animator on an animated TV series, on the other hand, may have to produce as much as 20–60 seconds per week, but at a lower quality. As you can see, these numbers vary widely depending on the material.

In addition to animator time, dozens of other factors need to be considered. How much time to write the script? Record the dialogue? Create the storyboards? Get approval from the network? Other factors may be technical, such as how much time it takes to render the project. If it takes three days to render all the frames, and the project is due tomorrow, you're dead meat. All these factors, plus many others, must be worked into a coherent schedule.

Developing a Schedule

Many factors need to be considered in creating a schedule. The best way to look at these factors is to put everything down on paper. Many producers use scheduling programs or custom spreadsheets to work it all out. Putting together a good schedule is a lot like putting together an assembly line—after one part of the process is complete, the next department picks up the work and adds to it. For example, you can't animate a character until it is built, so modeling and setup must happen before animation.

Some tasks can be overlapped. In a feature film environment, many studios develop and model the characters concurrently with the script and storyboard creation. This allows the animators to start work much sooner after the storyboard is locked. Rendering is another thing that can be overlapped. After a shot is finished, it can be rendered while the other shots are animated.

A simple schedule overlaps tasks for efficiency.

The best schedule interleaves all the required tasks seamlessly so that the film is completed cleanly and efficiently with no waiting around. Of course, all sorts of things that threaten to undermine the schedule are sure to pop up during production, but with a well-planned schedule, these can be accounted for much more easily. It's also good to add in a bit of cushion for those times when everything goes wrong. If the project is due in 10 weeks, perhaps create an 8-week schedule just to be sure that, when things slip, you still hit the final deadline.

How Much Will It Cost?

Money is always a big factor in creating animation. The general goal of a commercial project is to make the highest quality film for the lowest price. Animators are fairly skilled people, so they command relatively high wages. You can certainly hire less skilled artists, which affects quality. Hiring kids fresh out of school also is a way to save money, but many times these employees are not as productive as a skilled person. You tend to get what you pay for.

With the exception of high-budget feature films, cel-based animation production has moved overseas, mostly because it reduces the cost. This trend is also beginning to affect digital animation and affects production. When an animator in another country makes as little as 10% of what a local animator makes, the economics are pretty clear.

When a project goes overseas, however, you introduce language barriers and logistical problems, as well as quality-control issues. It is very difficult to communicate a creative vision to someone who is half a world away. This means storyboards and animation direction, for example, need to be crystal clear before they leave the local studio.

Other factors also need to be considered in estimating the costs, such as office space, electricity, equipment, and many others. This is where a good producer shows his or her salt in getting good deals on the ancillary things so the budget has room to offer more time and money to artists.

Making the Most of Your Budget

One of the best ways to get the most out of any budget is to know your medium. Knowing how and where to cut corners allows you to put most or all of your money on the screen.

Budgeting for Revisions

One great difficulty in budgeting a film is figuring out how to accommodate the thorny issue of revisions. Revisions usually come into play whenever you have one party communicating its artistic vision to another. It could be anything from an advertising agency telling a studio how it wants a character to look to an animation director telling animators how a character should move. Many times, the final product does not turn out to be exactly what was expected. Fixing it requires a revision. Revisions can take up nearly as much time as creating the original work, so you must plan for them. In contracts, you can specify a specific number of revisions to keep the fickle under control.

Story and Budget

Writers can easily create stories that are very rich, complex, and detailed. All they have to do is write more words. Ink is cheap; film is expensive. Unfortunately, in film, some ideas simply cost more to produce than others. In live action, a simple film with a handful of characters is a lot cheaper to produce than a big action blockbuster. The same goes for animation. The more characters, sets, and props a movie uses, the more time and money each minute of screen time is going to require.

This shot is framed fairly close, so it is cheaper to produce.

This shot includes much more scenery, so it is more expensive to produce.

Think about movies you've seen recently and how many different locations they used. Typically, the more locations there are, the more expensive the film. Animation is very similar. More locations mean more sets and more expense. Even the choice of shots affects budget. A long shot chosen over a close shot can even make a difference because you have to build more for the long shot.

Many writers and story people hate to be told that an idea is just too expensive to produce. But if you try to produce something that's too expensive to produce at the given budget, then corners must invariably be cut and the project is bound to suffer in terms of quality. It is much better to work from ideas that are achievable from the start.

Design and Budget

One way to address a budget is to design characters and props that meet the budget. If you design highly realistic characters, the audience will expect highly realistic animation. If you don't have the budget for this, quality will suffer. If your budgets are tight, it makes much more sense to design simpler characters. This way, the audience's expectations will not be so high.

This character will be more expensive to animate.   This character will be cheaper to animate.

Reuse and Budget

One way to lower budgets is to reuse characters, props, and backgrounds. This may not be possible for a single film, but it is very important for such things as a television series. Once a character is built, it can be used over and over. The only additional investment is animation time. The same goes for sets and props. Many series limit the number of sets, forcing writers to make do with the inventory at hand.

Making a Film

After you have a budget and schedule in place, it's time to start making the film. Whether you're doing a commercial film for a paying client or a low-budget film for yourself, the process of creating an animated film is pretty much the same.

Story and Ideas

I devote an entire chapter to this later in the book, but obviously, a film is nothing without a good story. Most of the time, you pitch and sell the idea to get the money and time to create the film. Once you have the idea sold, a development and refinement process probably takes place before the film actually gets made. This means refining the raw idea into a film that can actually be made. Many productions use almost as much time for story as they do for actual production time.

Script

Some animators argue that creating the script first biases a film toward dialogue and away from the visual aspects of animation. That is certainly a point, but this is not always the case. Some writers have a very good visual sense. In fact, a number of animation writers are also artists.

If the project is long form or requires a lot of dialogue, a script can be a very good start. Scripts are good for defining story structure, as well as major dialogue. Of course, as the script is visualized, things are likely to change.

Storyboard

Some productions choose to storyboard first. This makes a lot of sense in short-form films without much story structure or when the film has little or no dialogue. Many commercials are storyboarded. Storyboarding first tends to give you a film that is more visual. Storyboarding for a 3D film can be done the traditional way, with pencil and paper. It can also be done with rendered images you produced with a 3D program.

Modeling and Setup

Building and rigging the characters is a task that can start almost immediately. You are likely to know who the major characters are even before the story is finalized. In fact, you may need to create rough models of the characters to sell the project in the first place.

As the script and storyboard are finalized, you will have a much clearer idea as to what the modeling requirements will be. This enables you to model the secondary characters and props as the dialogue is recorded and the Leica reel is cut.

Dialogue

Once the script and storyboard are finished, it is time to record dialogue. Before you record dialogue, you need to cast your characters.

Casting your voice talent is one of the most critical tasks you face in making a film. If you can get excellent voice talent who give great performances, then you will have great raw material for animators to use in creating an inspired acting performance.

The voice determines, to a large degree, how the audience perceives a character, and you should make every attempt to get it right. You may have to hold many casting sessions, where you must audition a number of actors.

Casting Voices

Selecting voices for a film is like assembling players for a band. The individual voices must complement each other, yet they must all work together toward a common goal. Try to come up with a good mix of voices and textures. If two voices sound similar, it can get very confusing for the audience.

What does this character sound like? Casting a low voice will make him scary; casting a high voice might make him funny.

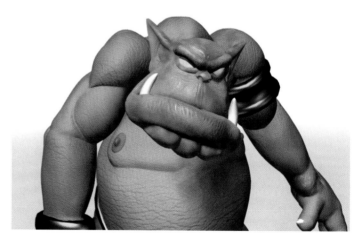

You should always go into a casting session with an open mind. Many times you won't know the voice until you hear it. If you have a preconceived notion of how you want your character to sound, it biases you against what could be a better solution. Actors are creative people, and they can bring a lot to the process. Give them a bit of rope to let them try and "discover" the voice. After they nail it, then let your directing skills kick in and fine-tune the performance.

When auditioning, listen to just the actor's voice, because that's all the audience will hear. It doesn't matter what the actor looks like; the sound is all that matters. A number of women perform voices for young boy characters, for example, but obviously could never play them onscreen. You're not casting the person, just the person's voice. Many directors look away from the person who is auditioning, so that the actor's gestures or appearance don't bias them.

If your budget is minimal, such as in a personal film, you may have to rely on friends or even perform the voices yourself. This doesn't have to be a problem; you can get a good performance from non-professionals as well. Aardman Animation has done some excellent films, such as *Creature Comforts*, among others, that use interviews with ordinary people as the dialogue track. People always sound more relaxed and natural when they're not trying to act and when they're talking about something personal.

Casting is difficult for the director but can be even more stressful for actors. Most of them will be rejected, and only a few will get jobs. Respect this when holding a casting session. With actors who don't make the cut, for whatever reason, be nice, and be sure to pass along a compliment or two as you let them down.

Recording Dialogue

After you cast the actors, you can go into the voice session to record your tracks. This is one of the more critical parts of the process, because a lousy voice track cannot be saved with great animation. Typically, a voice session is also one of the most fun parts of the process. You hear the lines for the first time, which is exciting. You also hear the jokes for the first time, which can be hilarious.

In a professional environment, the actors sit together in a booth, and a recording engineer operates the equipment. The director conducts the process, while various other people (producers, clients, etc.) usually gather and offer their sage advice, which the director may or may not take.

In a budget environment, try to get a decent recording however possible. This usually means getting good microphones and a quiet room. If you can, get a separate microphone for each actor.

Dialogue can be recorded one line at a time, or many lines can be recorded together, as in a radio play. Many times you have actors who voice multiple characters. In this case, you need to record lines individually. Recording lines one at a time makes editing much easier and allows you to introduce your own sense of timing on the final material.

If your dialogue is quick, with characters stepping on each other's lines, then you may need to record many lines in a single take. This can become tricky later, because it's much harder to edit this type of dialogue.

Directing Dialogue

The director needs to get the most out of each actor. This means communicating to the actors and letting them know what you expect. Before you record a scene, discuss it with the actors so they have an idea of how you see the action taking place. You also need to keep the actors fresh and spontaneous, so try to communicate your ideas quickly and concisely.

Be sure to get stands for the scripts, so the actors can keep their hands free. When recording, it's a good idea to get the actors into a creative flow, so they stay in character. Too many interruptions cause them to slip out of character, which just prolongs the process and makes the acting stale. Try to keep things moving along when everyone is in character. The first few reads of a script are usually the best. If you can't get the read you want, you may need to come back to it at the end of the session, so the actor has a fresh take.

Most directors like to have multiple takes, just to have a variety of material to choose from. The best way to do this and still keep the actors fresh is to have the actors record the same line (or lines) three times in a row, usually known as A, B, and C takes (which can also stretch into many more if needed). By saying the lines multiple times, actors can vary the reads each time and stay within character. As you record, mark down the take you like. If you're not sure, ask the engineer for a playback.

If an actor is not reading a line the way you want, the first temptation is to just read the line yourself to give the actor a hint. This is not a good idea, because actors need to find the lines themselves. If they simply parrot the director, the line is certain to fall flat. Try to get you point across in different ways by telling the actor the line needs to be louder, softer, subtler, angrier, nicer, more condescending, etc.

Ad-Lib

Some of the best voice actors are also very good comedians and improvisational actors. During the recording process, they may diverge from the script and throw in a few ad-lib lines. These can add a lot of spice and spontaneity to your film. On some productions, we've known our actors well enough to know that we can leave parts of the script open and allow them to fill in the blanks. You may also find that lines that looked great on paper just don't sound great when read. In this case, you may need to do a quick rewrite of the script in the recording studio or ask the actors to improvise something better.

Ad-libs and script changes, however, can be a real problem with clients and network executives. Most of the time, these people have already approved the script and expect any deviation from the script to go through another approval process. Be sure to record the original lines as well as the ad-libs, so you at least have a backup if the changes are rejected.

Keeping Track of Dialogue

With so many people involved in the recording process, it's a good idea to set up a system so everyone is on the same page. Each line in the script should be numbered, so the audio engineer has some sort of reference. During recording, you also need to keep track of the individual takes that you like. In live action, takes are numbered numerically (such as "Scene 3, take 5"), but many people in animation prefer to use alphabetic letters (take 3e) instead. This decision may be driven largely by the recording engineer's own preferences. Whatever method you choose, just make sure everyone knows.

Typically, the actors go through multiple takes during the session—perhaps dozens. After each take, the director indicates to the engineer which one is preferred. The director may also specify alternate takes as well. These are all compiled on a tape (or CD) for later. Try to pick only a few takes of each line before leaving the studio—you don't want to wade through a lot of unwanted material later. Don't be afraid of losing the other takes; the studio always keeps a backup that you can refer to if you want to.

Leica Reels

Once you have your storyboard and your dialogue, it's a good idea to cut a *Leica reel*, also known as an *animatic*. The Leica reel is still images timed to the dialogue and music. The finished Leica reel looks like a slide show that plays much like a rough version of your film. This tells you the length of each individual shot and also locks down the timing of dialogue.

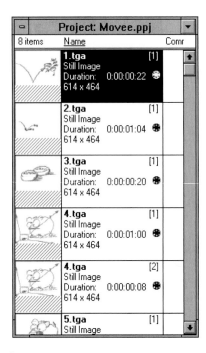

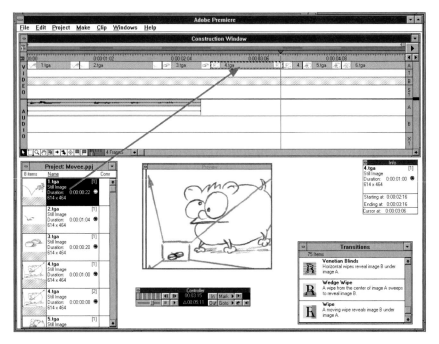

If you use Premiere to create your storyboard, simply load all of your scanned storyboard panels into the Project window.

Then drag these panels to the Construction window. If you have audio, drag that to the Construction window as well.

Creating a Leica Reel

On the desktop, a video editing package such as Adobe Premiere is a good choice for creating Leica reels. The procedure is relatively straightforward, and the principles apply to other editing packages as well.

First, you should get digital versions of your storyboard panels. If you created them in 3D, the files already exist. If the storyboard is hand-drawn, the drawings need to be scanned. For large storyboards, a scanner with a sheet feeder helps considerably.

To adjust the length of a storyboard panel, click on the edge of the panel's picture in the construction window and drag it right or left. The length of the panel appears in the Info window.

If you have dialogue, you also need to record the audio into your computer. Most recording studios can give you the dialogue as audio files on a CD, which can be copied to your computer's hard drive. If the audio is on tape, record the selected dialogue lines into your favorite sound editor one by one, making a separate little audio file for each line of dialogue.

Once you have all of your resources on disk, you first need to import the storyboard picture files into Premiere. If you have dialogue, import the sound files as well. If your animation is to video, set Premiere's timebase to 30fps; if your animation is timed to film, then 24fps is the proper timebase.

Now it's simply a matter of clicking and dragging the individual pictures to the video timeline and adjusting their lengths so that the film plays the way you want. In Premiere, when a still image is brought to the timeline, the default length is one second per image. By dragging the edges of the image on the timeline, you can add or subtract time to each panel.

If you have dialogue, it should be dragged to the timeline as well. Dialogue, however, is a fixed length—the only way to make it shorter is to cut words or sentences. As you work through the dialogue, you are also selecting the final takes from the recording session. You may need to jot down the exact parts of which audio tracks you are combining so the audio engineer has reference to help him match the tracks from the master tape.

After you've worked your way through all the dialogue and storyboard panels, render your Leica reel and watch it. If you need to, go back and make timing changes. You may also want to cut extraneous shots to tighten up the film, or add needed shots at this point. The finished Leica reel gives you a good idea of exactly how long your film will be, as well as exactly how long each shot in the film will be.

Layout

Once your Leica reel is finished, the timing and shot selection for the film are also locked down. It's finally time to start animation production in earnest. The production is likely to be building and rigging the primary characters and props long before the Leica reel is complete. Some productions may hold off on the secondary modeling because scenes can get cut during the animatic process. It makes no sense to build props for scenes that will never be animated.

Before the animators can begin animating, they need to have scene files that contain all the elements associated with the scene. This includes any characters, props, backgrounds, and audio, among other things. This task is sometimes called *layout*, but some studios call it *setup*. Technical directors usually perform the task, but animators also have been known to help lay out shots for animation.

Each layout varies depending on the requirements of the scene. If the animation involves a live-action composite, it may be as simple as placing the character in the shot and loading up the background plate. In a more complex shot, the artist doing layout may need to light the scene, rig characters, place props, and so on. The final layout should be a scene file that is ready to be animated.

A simple layout has the characters in the shot.

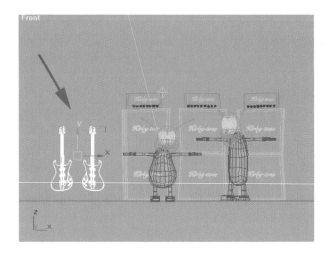

Notice how the props are off to the side so the animator can bring them in when needed.

Audio and Layout

When performing layout, don't forget the audio. Most animators need an audio track as reference, and it makes things a lot easier if they have the audio track already loaded in the scene file at the layout stage.

Audio can be managed one of two ways. First, you can create a separate audio file for each shot within the film. For example, if shot 6 starts on frame 251 and ends on frame 301, you create an audio file 50 frames long. That way, you simply load the file in your animation program and start animating. This puts a burden on the person who creates the audio files, which may number in the dozens.

A second, and more efficient, way of creating audio is to leave the dialogue as one continuous track, and adjust the start and end frames in the 3D scene file to match. In the preceding example, you'd simply set your start frame to 251 and end frame to 301. This saves a lot of time and effort.

Another advantage is that if you render your film as sequential still images (such as a Targa sequence), the images are numbered perfectly. Shot 6, for example, starts its numbering at 251. This ensures that your film will be assembled automatically as it's rendered.

Animation

After the scenes have been laid out, you're finally ready to actually animate your film. That's what most of this book is about, and animation is one of the truly fun parts of making a film.

When animating your film, the temptation is to animate every shot in sequential order, from beginning to end. This, however, is usually not the best way to proceed. The beginning of the film is very important to the rest of the film, so don't animate it until you are comfortable with your characters. This takes a while. The first shot you animate should probably be an easy one somewhere in the middle of the film. That way, you can get a feel for the characters before animating the critical shots. This also ensures that the end of your movie looks more fully resolved because it is animated at the end of production, when everyone has become most comfortable with the story, characters, and other elements.

Keeping Track of Things

After production begins laying out shots, you need to track each shot through the production process. It usually involves a bit of paperwork to ensure that everyone involved in production is kept up to date on the progress of the film.

Tracking Sheets

A tracking sheet is a piece of paper or Web page on a computer that keeps track of each and every shot as it flows through the production. It seems as though different studios call these documents by different names—lead sheets, production tracking, and so on. Despite the differing terminology, they all basically keep track of the same information.

Typically, tracking sheets are set up as tables. Each horizontal row contains the information for one shot. The vertical columns contain information for each step of the process. Typical columns might include modeling, texturing, rigging, layout, animation, and rendering. There may also be additional spaces for information such as the name of the animator, the number of revisions, and so on.

As each step is finished for each shot, the appropriate boxes are marked, so that the director and producers can instantly see the progress of the film.

File Naming Schemes

As soon as modeling begins, the production starts generating multiple files. These need to be managed, typically through some sort of file naming scheme. The schemes used vary by task, and many studios impose their own naming schemes that artists and animators must adhere to.

For tasks such as modeling and texturing, the files are usually not tracked by individual shot. These can be named by character or prop name. You may also place a production number on them, depending on the studio. When creating filenames, create a name, then tack on a revision number that increments sequentially. An example might be

Felix_model_006

One thing I always see people doing is adding words such as "final" to filenames (such as "Felix_Final") when they think the model or texture is finished. Invariably, there will always be one last revision, making the file named "final" not so final anymore. It's much easier to increment the revision number and be comfortable in the fact that the highest revision number is the most current version.

After layout starts, each file needs to be stamped with a strict naming scheme. Every production is different, but most need to track such things as production number, shot number, revision number, and the type of file. A typical naming scheme might look like this:

G107_027_LO_01

In the preceding example, "G107" is the production number, "027" is the shot number, and "01" is the revision. "LO" indicates that this file is a layout file with no animation. Once the animator sets keyframes, he changes the suffix when he saves the file, as follows:

G107_027_AN_01

If the animation in that shot is called for a retake, the animator ups the revision number, as follows:

G107_027_AN_02, G107_027_AN_03, and so on

As the animation is rendered, you should continue the naming scheme to the rendered files, as follows:

G107_027_RN_03.MOV

Note that "RN" has been substituted for "AN" to indicate this is a rendered image. I always find it much easier to keep track of things if the rendered filename is very similar to the animation file that created it. In this case, you can tell that it came from revision 03 of the animation.

Rendering and Output

Once your animation is complete, you need to render it and output to film or video. Film always looks great, particularly on the big screen. Unfortunately, you can't just hand people a 35mm print and tell them to go watch your film. Video is certainly a more practical medium, though it lacks the quality of film. You can also distribute your animation digitally on CD-ROM, DVD, or over the Internet.

Output to Video

Output to video is the most common output for computer animation. Video output cards are very reasonably priced, making it by far the cheapest way to get your film out to a format that people can see. You can simply print your video to a standard home video recorder, but this does not, by any means, give you the best quality picture. Digital decks that use the DV tape format along with an IEEE1394 interface produce excellent quality images.

Most post houses can also output your digital frames directly to the higher-end formats, such as DigiBeta, D1, and HDTV. You simply back up your frames to an archival medium such as CD-ROM or a DLT tape and have your post house do the conversion and output for you.

Output to Film

Film is a great medium for output. Videotape formats seem to change with the seasons, but 35mm film has been constant for almost a century. Many major studios even go as far as to record their digitally created cartoons to film for archive, even though film is not needed for broadcast.

If you want to output to film, you open up a whole new can of worms. Film requires images of much higher resolution. The typical film recorder requires an image that's at least 2048 lines wide, as opposed to video's 640 lines. Images at 2K resolution are ten times what's required for video and can blow your storage requirements through the roof. Not only that, but film recorders can be expensive to rent, as well. Some companies, however, have set up service bureaus and output film from your data on a per-frame basis.

To get your images to film, the typical process is to back up all the frames on an archival medium that the service bureau can read. DLT tape is the most popular format, because you can get over 40GB on a tape. After the tape is in the proper format, you basically hand it to the bureau, and they give you back a negative of your film and, of course, a bill.

Another way is to print your film to videotape, such as DigiBeta, and go to a service that prints video to film. This looks decent, but not nearly as good as a direct-to-film transfer. Some people are now using HDTV as the intermediate format. I've heard that this can work very well, particularly because HDTV can support 24fps.

There are other ways to get images to film. These are typically guerilla tactics, but they can work very well. One method is to print your film out at one frame per page on a standard color inkjet printer and then photograph the pages on a traditional animation stand. You would be surprised how good this can look. This method also gives you the option of using textured papers and drawing, painting, or further manipulating the printed frames by hand to give your digital animation a more natural look.

Another cheap way to output to film is to get a 16mm or 35mm animation camera and point it directly at your computer screen, photographing the images frame by frame. The big problem with this method is the refresh rate of your computer screen. Most computer screens refresh every 1/60 to 1/75 of a second. Unfortunately, this is very close to the average exposure time for movie film, which is typically 1/48 of a second or less. Using such short exposures generates flicker in your film. To avoid this, you need to make the camera's exposure time as long as possible—typically, a second or more. This way, you get a high number of screen refreshes for each frame, eliminating the flicker.

Adding Sound Effects

Now that your film has been animated and rendered, you still need to do some post-production to add sound effects and sync up the dialogue.

Creating good sound effects is an art in itself, and if you have the budget, a good sound engineer is worth the money. If you don't have that sort of budget, you can find plenty of sound effects CDs on the market with a wide variety of sounds, from realistic to cartoony.

There are also many times when you need sound effects that aren't in any collections. If this is the case, you need to create them from scratch. This basically involves setting up a microphone and recording the sounds you need. If you want the sound of breaking glass, for example, get a hammer and smash some pop bottles. (Wear safety glasses, of course!) You can be very creative in what types of objects you use to create your sound effects. Toys such as slide whistles, kazoos, and jaw harps make great sound effects. Also, atypical effects can make a scene much funnier. If a character runs into a wall, the sound of a bowling strike may be funnier than a simple thud.

One sound effect that is often overlooked is the ambient sound of the room. If you're in the city, the room may have the faint echoes of traffic in the distance. Country dwellers may have birds or crickets as their background. This type of effect is barely audible but adds a subtle sense of space to the film.

How do you add sound effects? Well, a good recording studio with an engineer is the best way to do this. Not only are you paying for the use of the studio's equipment, but you're also paying for the engineer's time and expert ear. If you can't afford this, most video editing packages allow you to add a track of sound effects over the dialogue and sync it to video. More sophisticated multi-track sound editing software packages are geared specifically for the task of mixing sound for film. These packages allow you to mix dozens of digital tracks in real time as well as add effects. The sound can then be mixed to a simple stereo or mono track and synced to your film in Premiere, or at a post-production facility.

Distribution

After your film is complete, how do you get people to look at it? Well, if the film was a work-for-hire project for a studio or commercial client, then that matter is pretty much out of your hands. The owner of the film handles the distribution.

If you have a student or a personal film, then distribution is very important. In the past, many people sent films to film festivals. There are a number of major festivals, including Annecy in France, the LA Animation Celebration, Hiroshima in Japan, as well as many, many more. Siggraph is a great festival for 3D animation.

One currently popular method of distribution is the Internet. Simply put up a Web site with a link to your film. Pass on the link to some of your friends. If they like it, they'll pass it on to their friends, and so on. Some films have really taken off through this word-of-mouth method. For more exposure, you might also consider a number of film sites on the Internet that take a cut of future proceeds to host your film.

CHAPTER 2

Story

In its most basic form, character animation is about storytelling. As you will see, characters drive a story, and in turn, the story further defines the character. A good story gives characters motivation, conflict, and a path of action. Without these things, your characters will not truly spring to life.

Knowing how to tell a good story will help your animation skills immensely. If you understand where a story is in any particular scene, then you will have a good idea of how each of the characters needs to act and behave to further the story. For those interested in making their own films, then having a good story is the first thing any filmmaker needs.

Characters and Story

The first step in creating animation is deciding what it will be about—in other words, the story. You will also need to decide what characters will be involved in this story. How you come up with the concept for the film will depend on a number of factors. Do you develop the story or the characters first?

You may already have a story you want to tell. In that case, you may need to develop the characters to tell the story. On the other hand, you may have a library of characters you have modeled and want to use. In this case, you may need to develop a story for those characters you're familiar with. A television series, for example, is written this way. The characters remain relatively constant, and the stories are tailored to them.

Wherever you decide to start, you will soon realize that story and character are very tightly coupled. The story you choose will help define the characters through their actions. Strong characters will, in turn, affect the story. Sir Lawrence Olivier as Hamlet plays much differently than Mel Gibson in the same role. Imagining a character such as Bugs Bunny in that role brings forth even more hilarious differences.

In order for a character to come to life, it will need motivation to make it do something and obstacles to make that task more interesting by causing conflict. These ingredients are also those of a good story.

Motivation Creates Character

In order for a character to do anything within a story, the character must be motivated. Characters are motivated by their needs. A little tramp is hungry and needs food. A powerful newspaper magnate needs money and power. Laurel and Hardy need to deliver a piano. What a character wants and needs determines who he is to the audience.

How characters pursue their needs gives the audience clues to their personalities. Perhaps two characters are running for the same political office. One pursues it honestly, the other one uses every trick in the book. They both need the same thing—political office—but their personalities cause them to go about it differently. Another good example might be the simple task of jumping over a puddle. Fred Astaire would do it gracefully, while Buster Keaton might trip and land flat on his face. Each character approaches the obstacle differently.

The character determines how the role will play. Should you cast this character as a hero or villain?

Obstacles Create Conflict

If you can identify what your characters need, then you can also create obstacles for them to overcome. This is what adds interest to the story. If Laurel and Hardy deliver the piano without incident, then the story falls flat. Place a very steep staircase in their way, and they have an obstacle to overcome. The comedy is derived from the many ways the piano can slip from their hands and fall down the stairs. Overcoming the obstacle of the stairs is what creates the comedy. Obstacles can be physical, such as in a staircase, but they can also take other forms. A character may need to overcome fear, for example. In any case, obstacles are the things that create conflict in a story.

Conflict Creates Drama

Stories are about conflict. A character simply walking down the street is not a story. It is also not very interesting. The character needs motivation—perhaps he is late and desperately needs to get to his wedding. If the street is littered with banana peels, then you have an obstacle, which creates conflict and the beginnings of a story. Does the character avoid the peels? Does the character slip? If so, when? Does he make it to the wedding, and in what shape? It is up to the storyteller to make the most of the situation.

Of course, larger conflicts can generate much more intricate and substantial stories. Complexity adds spice to a story. Still, you need to be sure your story line is clear and not overly burdened by being too complex. There should typically be one main motivation and conflict in the story, with a limited number of secondary conflicts to add interest.

For example, consider a simple story: A bumbling scientist creates a monster that escapes the lab and terrorizes the city. Unfortunately, he can't bear to kill his creation. This simple story has several conflicts. The main conflict is the scientist trying to overcome the love he feels for his creation, but secondary conflicts are many: finding a way to destroy the monster, not getting killed by the monster, etc.

Another example might be a wrongfully accused man who escapes from prison and must avoid the police while trying to clear his name. The conflict of keeping away from the cops is obvious, but the man's true motivation is proving his innocence. This is what drives the story. The cops and the chase simply add more obstacles and conflict to keep the story interesting.

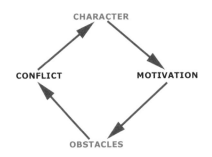

Stories are a circular thing. Characters are driven by motivations, and blocking the way are obstacles, which cause conflict, which further defines the characters.

The way a character handles conflict also gives the audience clues to his character. If the mad scientist can't kill his creation, it's because he has feelings of love for the creature. This, in turn, evokes empathy from the audience.

Conflict can also be much subtler. Many stories deal with internal conflicts—a character struggling with personal demons, growing up, or changing in some way. Internal conflict, however, will most likely manifest itself externally. An insecure character, for example, may act subordinate to a domineering spouse. The conflict is resolved only when the character confronts the insecurity and stands up to the spouse. In this case, the spouse represents the inner conflict. The events leading up to the confrontation are what tell the story.

Just as in war, when a conflict ends, there is resolution. This is the "payoff" to the story. In the case of *The Fugitive*, the real perpetrator is caught and our hero goes free. Or, he doesn't. Resolutions all too often take the form of "and they lived happily ever after." This might be nice for a children's story, but resolutions work best when the ending has a slight twist—one last surprise for the audience.

Exercise #1: Character Motivation

Go watch some movies. In each, try to determine the main character's motivation as well as the conflicts and obstacles that stand in the way. How does the character overcome the obstacles? What is the final resolution of the conflict?

Story Through Action

When writing a novel, an author can delve into the mind of a character to tell you what he or she is thinking. A line such as "Mary was happy with herself" could very easily be written into a novel with no problems at all. When writing a script, however, these sorts of statements can cause tremendous problems. We can't just say Mary is happy, we have to show it. How else will the audience know what she is feeling? They're not reading the script, they're watching a film. Mary will need to demonstrate her change of emotion through an action that the audience clearly sees.

How she demonstrates this emotion will also give the audience clues to her character. If she is a shy person, perhaps she will simply smile. A more gregarious Mary might jump for joy. Perhaps the moment could be covered with dialogue in addition to the action. Her actions are what define Mary to the audience. The story is told by exploring her character and how she changes.

Actions are what truly define characters. The audience does not know who a character is until that character moves and acts.

Visuals Come First

Film and animation are primarily visual mediums—the audience gets most of its information through what it sees. Studies have shown that visuals are more important than audio. If the audio contradicts the image, the image will win. Politicians have been known to use this fact with great results. If a politician is seen on the news in a visually appealing or patriotic setting, viewers think more positively about the politician, even if the news reporter's audio narration says negative things.

This is not to say that dialogue and audio are unimportant. Sound effects are very important. What a character says is extremely important. What the character does, however, is always most important. The image defines the sound, not the other way around. A line of dialogue such as "I'm so happy" will read straight if the character is smiling and acting happy. If the character acts sad as he says this, the image will win, and the audience will interpret the character as sad, ironic, or both. When writing a script for animation, you must take the visuals into account at all points.

If this character says "I'm so happy," the audience will think she is happy.

If this character says "I'm so happy," the meaning is unclear and the visual wins over the dialogue.

Developing a Story

As you can see, story structure has a few important concepts. First, you need a character who is motivated by a need. To achieve that need, the character must overcome obstacles. As the character deals with the obstacles, the audience learns more about who the character is. The concept is simple to explain, but telling a good story is an art form. Now that you understand some of the basic elements of storytelling, you can start to develop stories of your own.

What type of story do you create? There are quite a few. There's the simple story with a full plot that has a beginning, middle, and end. There are also stories that are really just a collection of gags strung together as in a Road Runner cartoon. Even those simple cartoons have the essential basics of a story—the Coyote's motivation is to catch the Road Runner. He just seems to encounter plenty of obstacles along the way.

Keep It Simple

While it is wonderful to imagine the most incredible and complex stories, there will always be limits. Even the biggest studio blockbuster has a fixed budget. For a personal film, the limit is the amount of time that you alone can give to the project. Most projects fall somewhere in the middle.

With any project, there is always the tendency to bite off more than you can chew. Creating a story is easy. Actually producing it is another matter altogether. It is always best to keep the time and budget constraints in mind. Knowing how much time and effort are required to produce a particular film is knowledge gained mostly from experience. The more films you make, the more aware you will be of the time and expense involved.

For students who are creating their first film, the best advice is to keep it small. This means sticking to a handful of characters and a situation that is manageable. Usually 2–3 minutes is plenty, 4–5 minutes ambitious. Films over 5 minutes might require some outside help. Remember, the classic Warner Bros. cartoons were all only 6 minutes long.

In any project, simplicity is typically the best way to go. Most of the best short films have very simple plots and stories. The Pixar shorts are a great example in that they all have only a handful of characters and one simple conflict. Another case for keeping a story simple and the number of characters small is that you can spend more screen time developing each character. Isn't "character" what character animation is all about?

Brainstorming a Premise

There are many ways to develop stories. Some people prefer to write out their thoughts. Some people like to work it out visually. One way is to simply brainstorm ideas. Brainstorming is an exercise in pure creativity. Get a sheet of paper and start writing down ideas. If you like to draw, you can also make simple sketches to work out a story visually.

Your story should have at least one character, one motivation, and one obstacle. It could be as simple as a child trying to open a child-proof container. Or, you could turn that idea on its head and have the adult incapable of opening the container, while the child, the dog, and even the pet hamster have it all figured out. A character could be extremely hungry, but food is hard to get. You could base your story on a traditional fairy tale—maybe the three little pigs who build houses out of straw, twigs, and bricks to avoid the wolf. If you want to add a strange twist to that concept, make them the three little lab rats who build mazes out of DNA to avoid the scientist. As you can see, the core idea of a film can be stated very simply in one or two lines. This simple statement is called a *premise*. Creating a good premise is your first step to creating a good film.

Exercise #2: Creating a Premise for a Short Film

This is a exercise in pure creativity. Take a sheet of paper and fill it with one-line premises for films. The more premises, the better, and if your ideas spill over to a second, third, or fourth sheet, that's great. You may even take several days to come up with the ideas, keeping a pad in your pocket to write down ideas as they hit you. At this point, you simply need to generate ideas for characters, stories, or both. These can be complete or incomplete ideas; the goal at this point is simply to free your mind, be creative, and come up with as many ideas as you can. Don't be afraid to even write down a seemingly bad idea. Sometimes a bad idea can give birth to a good one. This is not the time for left-brain editing; keep the process creative and strictly right brain.

continues

Exercise #2: continued

As you can see, these are just ideas, not complete stories, don't worry about whether or not they will work.

A sample page might look like this:

Adult can't open child-proof bottle.

Prank phone calls gone bad.

Angry milkman who delivers nothing but sour milk.

How to Climb a Tree—as told by a fish.

The Cockroach who became President.

Dust bunnies brought to life by static electricity.

The woman who stole the Eiffel Tower.

A hamster can't sleep because the dog is snoring.

A Drill Sergeant running a flower shop.

Plane with broken engine—two people—one parachute.

Ham and two slices of bread try to convince cheese to make a sandwich.

Hot potato—the world's sexiest potato.

Spinach on tooth that won't go away before big speech.

Stan, the guy who was canned as ham in Spokane.

Magician who has a stuck bunny.

Big mean wrestlers playing shuffleboard.

Put these ideas away for a day or two, and then go back and review them objectively. For each premise, try to picture exactly how the story will take shape. Remember a complete story needs three things: character, motivation, and obstacles.

To see if your premise has promise, you might expand the basic concept on paper, even go as far as to sketch out ideas for gags or situations. If the story points flow readily, chances are the premise is sound. If you can't picture how the premise will be made into a film, then put that idea aside for another time or another film. That discarded idea could be a valuable reference for a future project.

Ultimately, one of these many ideas will strike you as the idea for your film. Once you've chosen your premise, you'll need to develop your story.

Developing Your Premise into a Story

As you can see, the possibilities for premises are only limited by your imagination. Once you have a premise in hand, you need to ask yourself some very serious and objective questions about how the film will be made.

The first question you need to ask yourself is if the film can be made at all. If it's a story about fish, for instance, you may need to animate water. If you do a story about a barber, you may need to animate realistic hair. Ask yourself if your software is capable of handling the types of shots and characters the premise demands. If not, you may want to choose another premise or put the premise into another setting.

You also need to think about length. Some stories cannot be told in a few minutes, though you'd be surprised as to how much you can cram into that span of time. Many commercials tell great little stories in 30–60 seconds. Simple is usually better, however. Typically, this means focusing on one set of characters, one motivation, and one set of conflicts.

One way to flesh out your story is by going through another brainstorming session to generate as many ideas related to the story as possible. Write down these ideas on note cards, so you can keep track of them and arrange them into a story.

If your premise is good, you can generate plenty of ideas, in fact, way too many to fit within your time constraints. The problem may be one of too many ideas, in that almost half the cartoon has to be eliminated. Throwing out good material is always painful.

If you have too much material, you can think of it as either a luxury or a curse. If deleting the extra material from your story makes it incomprehensible, then your story might be cursed with too much complexity. You probably need to take a step backward to rethink the premise or the major story points to get the film to a manageable length. If you can toss out material and still have a sound story, then you have the luxury of too much good stuff. Keeping only the best material will make your film that much stronger. Even if you have lots of great material, don't delude yourself into thinking it all needs to be put in the film. Every extra bit of material means an extra animation for you to complete. If you bite off more than you can chew, it can come back to haunt you later.

Exercise #3: Fleshing Out Your Premise

You'll need a stack of note cards or Post-It notes for this exercise. Select your favorite premise from the previous exercise. Using the premise as your guide, think up story points, writing down or drawing each point on a separate card. These points can be as simple as "She walks down the street" and "Notices something in the window." If you have an idea for a visual gag, draw it on the card. You should simply generate a large number of ideas at this point. If the ideas don't flow readily, you might want to select a different premise.

Once you have as many ideas as you can think of, go through the stack of cards and organize the story points into a rough outline of the story. You can do this by pinning the cards on a bulletin board or laying them out on a table. Once you've arranged these cards into an outline, you have a good idea of what your story will look like.

Here's a simple example:

IDEA — HAMSTER CAN'T SLEEP

Hamster curls up in his wheel with blanket & pillow.

Dog snores—shakes house.

Hamster puts clothespin on dogs nose.

Dog's head swells up, blowing off clothespin like a bullet.

Hamster fills dog's head with laundry.

Laundry comes out pressed and folded.

Hamster encases dog's head in cement.

Dog rolls over, crushes Hamster with cement head.

Hamster cuts dog's head off.

Removed head snores, Body snores, too.

Etc.

Developing a Script

Once you have a ton of ideas, you'll have a stack of note cards and will need to organize your story so that you know, beat for beat, the exact sequence of events, including the ending. Let's take the idea of the adult who can't open the childproof bottle. Getting to the contents of the bottle is the adult's motivation; the complex cap is the obstacle. Pretty simple story.

Fleshing out the story, the adult could use all sorts of wild schemes to get the cap off—a can opener, a blowtorch, dynamite. If other characters such as a kid, a dog, and a hamster manage to open the bottle with no help, it can just serve to humiliate the adult and strengthen his motivation. He sees that his goal is possible.

Organizing the story means that you need to build the gags, one at a time. A simple structure might be alternating the adult's attempts with those of the other characters. The adult tries opening the bottle by hand, gives up, and then the child comes in and opens it. This motivates the adult further, who resorts to more drastic measures. These fail, and then another character opens the bottle. The adult's battle with the bottle escalates further, and so on.

All these conflicts need to build to an ending as well. The ending could be simple with the adult driving himself crazy with frustration. It could be ironic—he finally opens the bottle, only to find it empty. It could be a bit more fantastic—he has such a pounding headache that his head explodes. You could make a surreal *Twilight Zone* ending, where the adult and his world are themselves contained within another giant childproof bottle. Again, there are an infinite number of twists and possibilities to any story.

As you finalize the structure of your story, you will also need to be writing a script. This could be as simple as a point-by-point outline of the action, to a full script with dialogue and screen direction.

Dialogue

As you write the script, you may also find it necessary to add dialogue. It is certainly not a requirement, as many of the best cartoons have no dialogue whatsoever. Dialogue does help considerably in defining your characters. A good script and voice performance will help your characters appear real and make their personalities pop off the screen. A good voice track is also great for animators, who can use it to guide the performance.

If you decide to add dialogue to your film, then you will need to hone your writing skills. Writing dialogue that sounds natural and unforced can be difficult. There are a couple of handy hints that might make the process easier. First, listen to real conversations, perhaps even put them on tape and transcribe them to see how they work. You'll notice that people tend to speak in short sentences or fragments, many times interrupting each other. Another way to get a sense of dialogue is to imagine a character as a famous personality. If he's a tough guy, for example, does he talk like Robert DeNiro, Humphrey Bogart, or Marlon Brando? Using a famous character's speech patterns as a guide is a good way to get started with the writing process. Hopefully, the character will take a life of his/her own and diverge from the guide. If you base your character on a famous personality, however, you will need to be careful with voice casting—don't have your actors imitate the voice as well. (Unless, of course, you're doing parody.)

One problem that happens time and time again is too much dialogue. Long stretches of dialogue can eat up valuable screen time. Unless the dialogue is extremely well directed and acted, it can also drag down the quality of a film. While it is not a hard-and-fast rule, most animation benefits from short, snappy dialogue. A sentence or two per character is usually all that is needed to cover the action and keep the film moving along. It is also easier to direct and animate. If a character needs to speak paragraphs, it had better be for a very good reason. One rule of thumb in live action is that the audience's attention span is only about 20 seconds. Try listening to any speech that goes on for more than that without drifting. Since animation usually moves along faster than live action, the attention span is even less.

Exercise #4: Scripting a Story

Now that you have a simple story, write it up as a script. Be sure to include any dialogue that you've created for the characters.

Visualizing Your Story

At this point, in addition to writing the script, you'll need to be visualizing as well. Animation is a very visual medium, so you will absolutely need to see how your film looks on every shot. Even if you draw in stick figures, sketching out your ideas in storyboard form will help you understand exactly how gags and situations in your film will be staged.

The key here is to block out the film, not make pretty pictures. Accuracy to the look of the characters is less important at this stage than composition and flow of the film as a whole. As long as the storyboard conveys the idea, it doesn't matter what it looks like—especially if it is only for your own use. It is also easy to fall in love with the drawing of a bad shot because of the time investment. If a client needs to see "clean" boards, do them after you've worked out the details.

When creating the boards, it is also a good point to look for holes in the story, or possible gags. You may find that certain gags that sounded great in your script don't work visually, and it is much better, and cheaper, to make that cut now, rather than when the film is complete.

While sketching storyboard panels can be very quick for some people, others have problems with drawing. Drawing 3D characters might be less accurate, as the drawings might not be true to the actual characters. If your characters are already built, you can visualize the story another

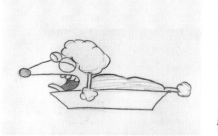  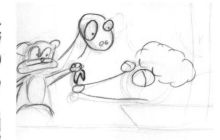

These storyboard panels are simply drawn.

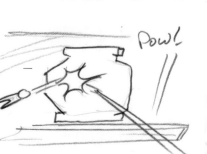 

way, without drawing. Simply pose the characters in your 3D application, and render stills to use as the storyboard. No scanning is required, the images are true to the actual characters, and the 3D scene files can be saved and used later as layouts for animation.

These panels were created by posing the characters in a 3D package. The panels are a bit more true to the characters.

Exercise #5: Storyboard Creation

Create a storyboard for the idea you've been developing. Work out order of shots, as well as the flow of the film. Don't worry too much about neatness on the first pass—just get the idea across however you can. Once you're satisfied with the storyboard, go ahead and clean it up and number the shots.

Finalizing Your Story

Once you have your story worked out, you're only at the first step. The film still needs to be produced. As a story is produced, minor things may change, but the core of the story should remain the same. You should have a good story, which is the foundation for creating a good film.

Conclusion

Creating stories is an art that every animator needs to know. As the "actors" in the story, the animators are the ones who are actually "telling the story." Understanding how stories work helps your animation skills immensely. Write some stories on your own using the techniques outlined in this chapter. Practicing the art of creating stories makes you a better storyteller.

CHAPTER 3

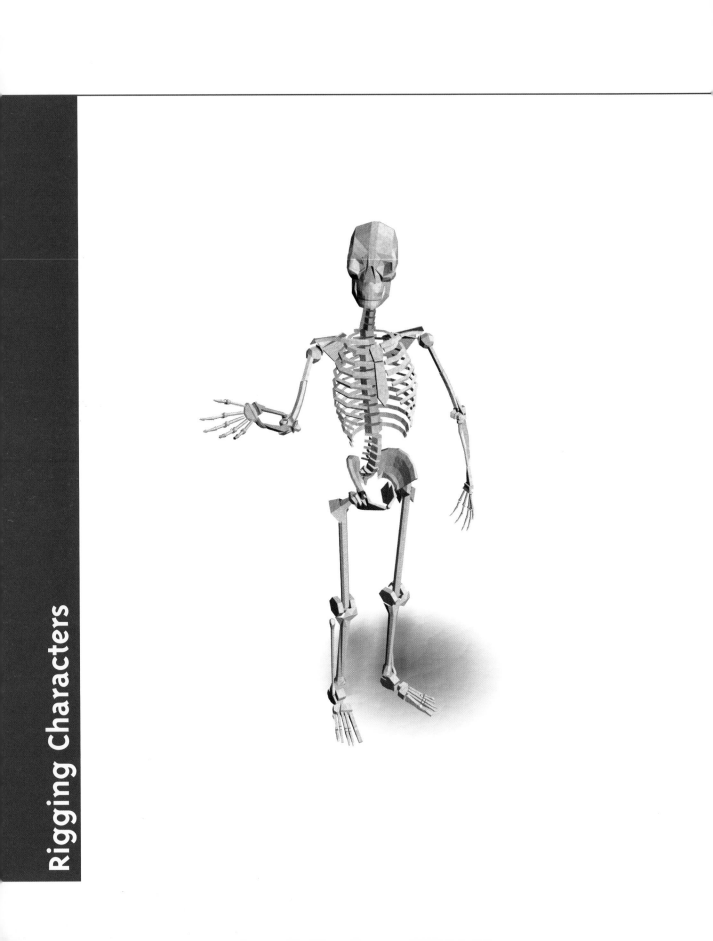

Rigging Characters

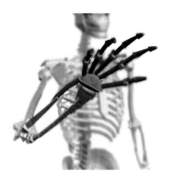

R igging is the task of setting up a model for animation. (Some of the basics of this were covered in *Volume I*). Basic rigging involves building a skeleton and skinning the character. The primary goal of rigging, however, is to make it as direct and easy as possible for the animator to do the job. Ideally, the character needs to be animated as quickly as the animator can think. This may seem to be a daunting task.

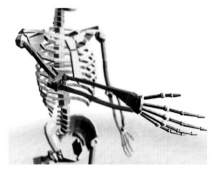

A good character rigger is part animator, part programmer, and part interface designer. The rigger needs to understand how animators work and translate that into an efficient setup. The perfect setup allows animators to have extensive control over the character while it also automatically manages those parts of a character that the animator does not need to think about.

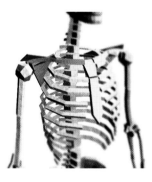

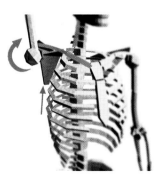

Sliders

One of the most common techniques for rigging a character is to create sliders. A slider is an object in the scene that controls the action of other objects. For a simple example, think of the many joints in the spine. Rather than select and rotate each individual joint, you can use a slider to rotate all the joints at once. Creating a slider is fairly straightforward; it involves simply connecting the action of one object to another.

These sliders control the character's facial shapes.

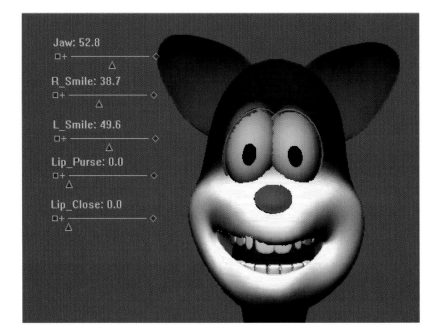

Automation

Another common rigging trick is to automate certain parts of the character. One commonplace example of automation is IK. IK automatically rotates the many joints in a chain so that they always meet a specific goal: the IK handle. Moving the handle automatically rotates the joints.

Other forms of automation may be more specific. A character's forehead may wrinkle when the brows are lifted. The muscles may bulge as the arm is flexed. These sorts of behaviors can also be created by connecting the actions of one part of the body to another.

Note

When automating a skeleton or creating sliders, many times you need to create custom attributes. A number of packages allow you to create custom attributes for objects within a scene. These are variables, or numerical values, that you can add to an object. These attributes, however, are names only. Adding a "smile" variable to a head doesn't instruct the character to smile. You still need to connect the attribute of "smile" to the morph shapes that make the character smile.

Automation can also be taken further, to actually animate parts of the character automatically. One example is to keep the hips centered between the feet. This sort of automation, however, begins to encroach on the animator's turf, so you need to be careful how far you take it.

Wiring Things Together

The real key to creating sliders and automation is how you connect the actions of one part of the character to another or to a slider. Some people refer to this as "wiring." How you wire a character depends, to some degree, on the individual package that you're using. Most tools, however, fall into several broad categories.

Direct Relationships

A direct relationship is the easiest way to connect the actions of one object to another. A direct relationship says A = B. The two values could be anything, such as the linear motion of the slider controlling the rotational motion of an eyelid, for example.

Some packages have nice graphical interfaces for setting this up. If this is not the case, a very simple expression can perform the same function. Expressions are covered later in this section.

Set-Driven Keys

The concept of set-driven keys was initially developed for Alias|Wavefront's Maya, but similar techniques have appeared in other packages as well. A set-driven key takes the concept of direct relationships one step further by allowing you to alter the relationship between objects based on a user-defined curve.

For example, if you want the eyelids of a character to stop rotating once they are closed, a set-driven key enables you to limit the rotation. A really complex example might be tying all the joints involved in a walk to a slider. Moving the one slider moves the character through the walk cycle. Adjusting the rate of the slider varies the rate of the walk. Although this might not be a very practical application, it does demonstrate the power of this technology.

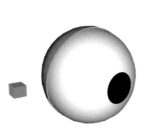
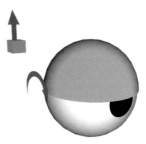

The box in this scene acts as the slider.   As the slider moves, the lid rotates.

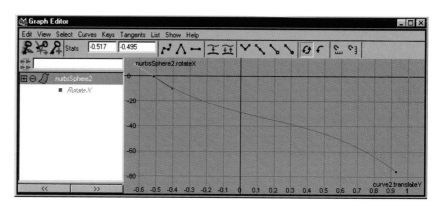

In a set-driven key, this motion is controlled by a curve.

Expressions

Expressions are used to automatically connect parts of a scene or a character. Rather than a keyframe, an expression is substituted, which automatically calculates the animation data every time a new frame is encountered. Expressions can be used for anything from the simple task of making one object follow another to very complex systems that create virtual control panels for your characters.

Expressions are very powerful tools. They can be used to create complex motions, and so can ease the load on the animator. They can also create relations between different parts of a character, so that when you move one part, the others follow along—such as with the many joints in a spine. People using expressions need to be careful, however, because a character can very quickly become over-automated, so that it is difficult to control and loses its natural feel. Expressions are at their best when they help, but not hinder, the animator.

It's Only Math

Expressions do use math. That may be a bit intimidating for some, but with expressions, a little bit of math can go a long way. Many common expressions don't use anything more complicated than addition and multiplication. A basic knowledge of trigonometry should be the most math any character setup person would ever need, though those with programming backgrounds are certainly at an advantage in this area. Although many of the larger studios have people dedicated to writing expressions and setting up characters, it makes a great deal of sense for every animator to understand the basics of expression writing.

Software Differences

Some software does not support expressions at all, though most of the better packages do in one form or another. Creating expressions is very specific to the particular package you are using. The syntax of the expressions is different for each package, so you must be willing to open your manuals to understand what your package requires. This book tries to take a product-neutral stance, so it includes generic expressions rather than expressions written for one type of package.

Expressions also expose, to a certain degree, the inner workings of your software package. It's a very good idea to understand how your own software works to get the most out of the expressions you write. Again, this means reading the manual and asking questions.

Variable Types

When working with data in a 3D scene, you come across two basic data types: scalar and vector.

Scalar Variables

A scalar variable contains a single value. This can be anything that can be represented by a single number—the X position of an object, the radius of a sphere, the transparency of an object, and so on. For example, the position of an object might be represented by a set of three scalar variables.

POSITION.X = 5

POSITION.Y = 2

POSITION.Z = 7

RADIUS = 32

Some software also distinguishes among different types of scalar variables, separating them into distinct categories:

- Float variables contain a floating point number, such as 3.1415 or −32.6754.

- Integer variables contain only whole numbers without decimal points, such as 1, 67, −364, and so on. These are usually used for attributes that cannot have fractional values, such as the number of subdivisions in a sphere.

■ Boolean or binary variables are either on or off. Most software packages use the number 1 for "on" and 0 for "off." These variables are used for attributes that are either on or off, such as the visibility of an object.

Vector Variables

Some packages also support vectors, which are used to represent a set of three-dimensional values. Rather than use separate scalars, such as POSITION.X, POSITION.Y, and POSITION.Z, you specify POSITION, a value that contains the three scalar values.

So, rather than use three equations

$$POSITION.X = 5$$

$$POSITION.Y = 2$$

$$POSITION.Z = 7$$

you substitute the vector value

$$POSITION = [5, 2, 7]$$

This assigns the numbers accordingly.

The equation

$$POSITION \star 5$$

multiplies all the X, Y, and Z values by 5.

In practice, however, most expressions for characters tend to segment out the X, Y, and Z components. For example, you may want an expression that affects only the rotation of an eyelid along on axis, such as in a blink. In this case, it's better to use scalars.

Simple Expressions

To get things started, the following sections provide a few simple expressions that use a set of cubes.

Direct Relationships

The simplest expression allows one object to control another. This is the same equation as A = B, and sets up a direct relationship as discussed earlier. For example, if you have two cubes, and you want one cube's X rotation to match the other's, you can write something like

$$CUBE\_A.rotationX = CUBE\_B.rotationX$$

After the expression is entered, CUBE_A's rotation mimics CUBE_B's rotation exactly.

Offsets

An offset is a constant numeric value added into the expression. The number is mostly used to offset or align two objects.

In the case of the cubes, if you want them to always be 45 degrees apart, you write something like:

CUBE_A.rotationX = CUBE_B.rotationX **+ 45**

Multipliers

Another simple use of expressions is to make one object move in multiples of the other. For example, if you want one cube to rotate twice as fast as the other, you multiply by 2.

CUBE_A.rotationX = CUBE_B.rotationX *** 2**

If you want it to rotate half as fast, divide by 2.

CUBE_A.rotationX = CUBE_B.rotationX **/ 2**

Or multiply by .5.

CUBE_A.rotationX = CUBE_B.rotationX *** 0.5**

Creating Sliders Using Expressions

Making cubes spin around in space is fine and dandy, but you need to be able to apply this to characters. The most direct use of an expression is in the creation of a slider. Here's a simple eye with a clamshell eyelid.

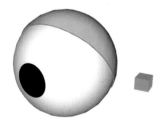

Take a simple eye, consisting of a sphere with a hemisphere as the eyelid. To open and close, this eyelid rotates around its X axis.

Create a dummy object within the shot to be the slider. Name the slider "LidSlider."

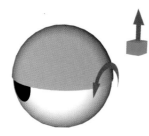

Moving the slider vertically along the
Y axis rotates the lid.

Create an expression for the eyelid similar to this:

$$EyeLid.rotation.X = LidSlider.translation.Y$$

You may find that you have a scaling problem. If your software measures rotation in degrees, for example, you may need to move your slider 180 units just to close the lid. This is where a multiplier comes in handy. Divide the expression by 180 to amplify the action of the slider.

$$EyeLid.rotation.X = LidSlider.translation.Y/180$$

If this is too much amplification, reduce the divisor accordingly.

As you can see, creating a slider is a matter of nothing more than creating a very simple expression.

Scripting

Scripting is similar to expressions, but goes a step further to offer up a fully functional programming language. Some packages even offer industry standard languages such as Java, LISP, and BASIC. Having a programming language gives the character rigger a huge palette of tools to draw from. Of course, this book is not a programming manual, so the hard core programming lessons will be left to another book.

One place where scripts do come in handy is in creating macros, or sequences of commands that can be stored and called up at will. These are helpful if you find yourself repeating the same series of operations over and over.

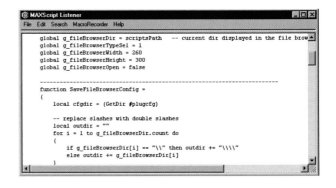

Scripting is much like programming
and can get quite complex.

Skeletal Setups

When rigging a character, the first order of business is to get the skeleton working. The goal is to make the character easy for the animator to manipulate.

Grab Points and Handles

Skeletal animation is much easier when you make it simple for the animator to easily select parts of the character. This is typically done by creating null objects that are placed as "handles" or "grab points" for the animator to use in manipulating the character. In addition to nulls, some people use locators; others use non-rendering text objects because they're self labeling. Any type of non-rendering object will suffice. In stop motion, a grab point is a hard point on a clay character that the animator can grab to move a joint without seriously deforming the clay. Grab points are used on digital characters but in a slightly different context.

The feet and legs are a good example of where grab points come in handy. You can use the IK handles created by the software to manipulate the legs. These handles, however, are usually buried within the character's mesh and can be hard to locate. To make it easier on the animator, you can create a grab point that is outside the mesh and easy to find. Moving the grab point moves, in turn, the IK handle.

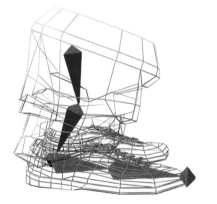

With the skeleton buried under the mesh, it's hard to see the ankle, much less select it.

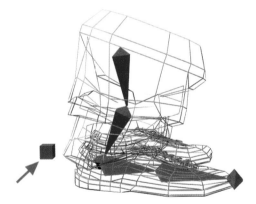

Creating a grab point outside the mesh makes it much easier to select the ankle.

Creating a Grab Point

The software you are using affects—to some degree—how you create a grab point. Usually a null object is used as the grab point. Some people choose to use text objects because the text can give the animator information. For example, you could use "RF" and "LF" to indicate the right and left foot, respectively.

The object is then connected to the IK handle on the ankle. The easiest way to make that connection is to simply make the grab point the parent of the IK handle. This allows you to translate, but problems may occur if you need to rotate the IK handle, because the handle rotates around the center of its parent. The way to fix this is to move the parent's pivot point to match that of the IK handle.

Another way to create a similar effect is with a point constraint. This gives you pretty much the same functionality as creating a parent-child relationship, but without the hierarchy. After the grab point is created, the animator has an object that is easily accessible from any viewport.

Setting Up a Foot

The foot always presents problems when creating a manageable skeleton. The big problem is the way the foot rolls along the ground. The foot can pivot on any one of three points: the heel, the ball of the foot, and the toes.

Here's one way to use a series of nulls, a grab point, and a simple hierarchy to control the foot. It's been tested in 3ds max and Maya.

This setup gives you three IK handles: one each at the heel, the ball of the foot, and the toe.

The foot can pivot at three points.

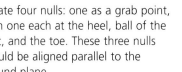

Start with a simple skeleton. The leg is a two-joint chain, whereas the foot bone and toe bone are single-joint chains. Make sure these all exist in the same hierarchy.

Create four nulls: one as a grab point, then one each at the heel, ball of the foot, and the toe. These three nulls should be aligned parallel to the ground plane.

Link the IK handle to its respective null.

Make the grab point the parent of the heel.

Make the heel the parent of the toe.

Finally, make the toe the parent of the ball of the foot.

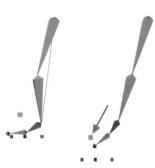

That's it. Lifting and moving the grab point moves the foot.

If the ankle goes beyond the IK limit, the foot naturally bends to compensate.

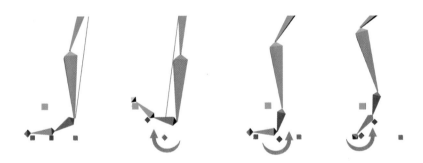

Rotating each of the other three nulls rotates the foot around each pivot point.

Refining the Foot

The setup described in the preceding section is pretty nice, and it offers a good degree of control. But you still need to select as many as four different objects to manipulate the foot. This can slow down the animator in two ways: First, the animator needs to select different objects. Second, the animator needs to switch from translation to rotation to pivot the foot.

Another solution is to create three sliders near the grab point: heel roll, ball roll, and toe roll. These attributes can be connected to the rotation of the foot in much the same way as the eyelid was connected to a slider earlier in the chapter. That way, the animator can always stay in translate mode and not have to select new objects.

Spine Setup

The spine contains dozens of vertebrae and can be a real pain to animate. To simplify the animation process, most animators don't create a bone for every vertebra in the spine. You can use as few as three to over a dozen. The more spinal joints you use, the more accurate the deformations, but the more complex the setup.

One of the key tricks to setting up a biologically correct spine is keeping the pivot points of the spine as close to the back of the character as possible. The joints in the spinal column of a human run along the back. In addition, they pivot toward the back of the joint.

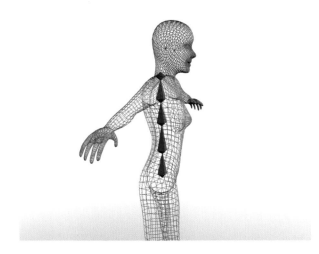

This spine is biologically incorrect because it runs through the center of the torso.

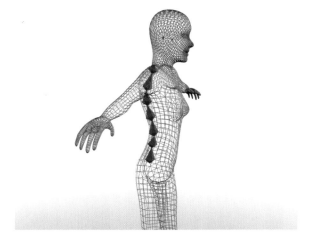

This is much better, and the resulting character will look more natural.

Because there are so many joints in the spine, it is usually a good idea to create sliders to control its bend. Tying the rotations of the many spinal joints to one controlling object can do this quite easily and can simplify the animator's work.

Create an object to control the spine.

Select the first joint of the spine. Connect the X rotation of the spine to the X rotation of the object. Do the same for the Y and Z rotation. Rotating the object should rotate this joint.

Repeat this for the rest of the joints of the spine. Manipulating the control object should manipulate the spine.

Ribs

Some animators go as far as to create skeletal ribs for their characters. This does complicate the setup, but it has the advantage of keeping the upper torso fairly rigid while allowing the belly to remain flexible. Setting up the chest in this manner can also help a character breathe realistically, which is essential for creating a believable character.

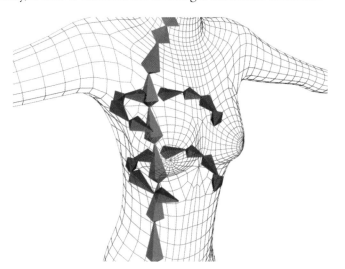

Creating ribs has the advantage of keeping the upper torso rigid.

Shoulders

A simple shoulder can be created with one bone running across the top of the spine so that the arms connect to its ends. For many types of characters, this sort of setup serves perfectly well. Those wanting to create a truly realistic character, however, need to construct a more accurate skeleton.

In real life, the shoulder is a complex series of joints that center around the actions of the scapula (shoulder blade) and clavicle (collarbone). The interactions of these bones affect the way the skin deforms on a character.

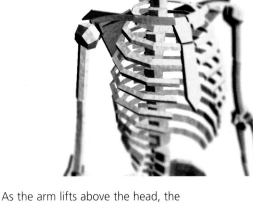

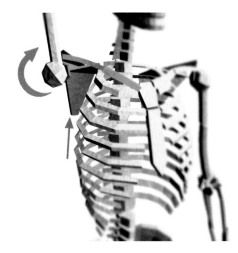

As the arm lifts above the head, the clavicle and scapula lift as well.

Creating this same effect in a skeleton can be a bit tricky. One way is to create a scapula that follows the action of the clavicle. This way, the scapula can affect the underlying deformation of the skin more accurately. The scapula can be a bone that is linked hierarchically to the clavicle. As the clavicle animates, the scapula follows. A more complex setup would involve creating a set-driven key to mimic the precise action of the scapula.

Forearms

The forearms also consist of two bones. Most skeletons use only one forearm bone, and this is fine for most applications. In real life, however, the forearm consists of the radius and ulna. The radius is the bone that ends along the thumb side; the ulna is the bone that terminates on the pinky side of the hand. Creating a separate radius and ulna bone for the skeleton allows for much more realistic deformation.

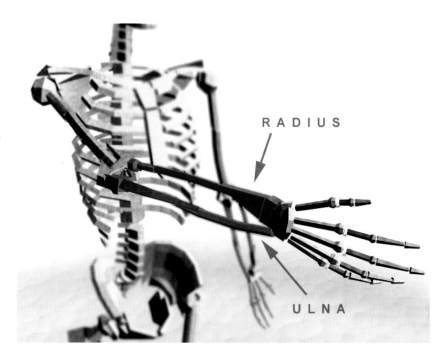

The radius is the bone that ends along the thumb side; the ulna is the bone that terminates on the pinky side of the hand.

RADIUS

ULNA

The one catch in creating separate radius and ulna bones is when you want to use IK, which requires a single bone from the elbow to the wrist. The simplest way to set this up is to reserve this "forearm" bone for IK—it does not deform the mesh. Then create two additional bones: the radius and ulna, which are drawn in the opposite direction to the forearm bone.

Take a standard left arm with a two-joint chain. The box at the end of the chain represents the palm of the hand.

Create two single joint IK chains; name them "radius" and "ulna." These are drawn in the opposite direction as the forearm.

Link both the radius and ulna to the humerus at the elbow, and then link the IK handles of the two bones to the palm of the hand.

Position these so the radius runs from the elbow to the thumb and the ulna runs from the elbow to the pinky.

That's it. Rotating the palm causes the radius and ulna to behave in a realistic manner.

Hands

Hands are very complex structures; a typical hand has a dozen joints in just the fingers. Like the spine, the many joints of the fingers make an ideal place to use sliders for simplifying the process.

Before we jump into making sliders, it's a good idea to observe how the hand moves. In most situations, the pinky bends first, then the ring finger, then the middle finger. The index finger can follow these but is usually more independent, such as when pointing. This leads to a very simple setup that involves only two sliders. In this situation, the joints of the fingers are aligned so that X rotation is along the plane of the hand and Y rotation is perpendicular to the plane.

A simple hand skeleton.

Select the joints in the pinky. Connect the X rotation of these joints to the first slider.

Manipulating the slider bends the pinky.

Select the next finger. You need to tie the X rotation to the same slider. Remember that the rotation of this finger should lag behind that of the pinky.

This can be accomplished in a number of ways. If you are using set-driven keys, then extend the rotation curve of this finger so that it lags behind the pinky.

If you are using expressions, then multiply the entire expression by a fractional number, such as 0.8, which reduces the ring finger's rotation to 80% that of the pinky.

The same procedure happens for the middle finger, except that its X rotation is reduced even further.

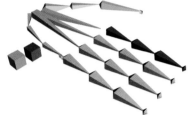

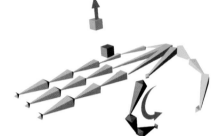

The last three fingers are linked to the first slider.

The index finger gets its own slider, much like that of the pinky.

Connect the X rotation of the three index finger joints to the slider using an expression or a set-driven key.

To create a slider that controls the spread of the fingers, first take the index finger and connect its Y rotation to the slider.

The middle finger is connected in the same way, except that its rotation is reduced by 50%. If you're using set-driven keys, dampen the curve. If you are using expressions, multiply the expression by 0.5.

The ring finger needs to rotate in the opposite direction. If you are using expressions, multiply by −0.5 to get the proper motion. If you are using set-driven keys, reverse the curve so that it moves in the negative direction.

The pinky's motion is exactly opposite that of the index finger, so multiply the expression by −1.0, or adjust the curve accordingly.

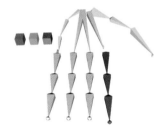

The final slider controls the spread of the fingers. The trick here is that the first two fingers rotate one way; the last two rotate the other way.

After the slider is set up, it spreads the fingers naturally.

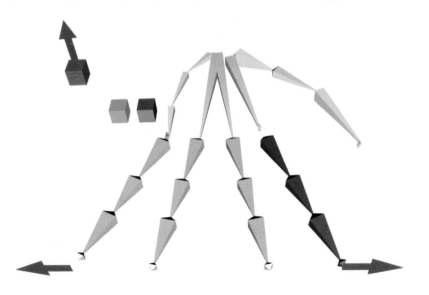

This setup is good for most general hand motions, such as gestures used in conversation. If the motions get complex, such as when the character is playing piano, then you need to make the sliders a bit more complex. In that case, you might want to use individual sliders to curl each finger and a single slider to control the spread of the fingers.

Facial Rigging

Most facial animation is usually done using multi-target morphing, and most packages automatically create a nice little panel of sliders to control this process. For many people, this is a perfectly good interface to use when animating. If you want, you can certainly tie the morph targets to custom sliders to make interaction more convenient.

The Jaw

Most people use morph targets to manipulate the jaw. The problem with morph targets is that they don't take into account the fact that the jaw has the ability to move from side to side. This can lead to suspiciously symmetrical facial animation.

One way get around this problem is to create three distinct facial poses to open the mouth: one with the jaw centered, and one each with the jaw left and right. Animating this can be a bit sticky, because when animating the jaw from left to right, you can very easily stretch the lower face. You should be aware of this pitfall as you animate and use only one of the three poses at a time.

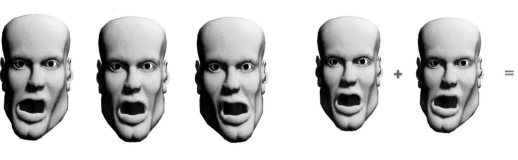

To get side-to-side jaw motion, you can create three individual morph targets.

However, if you mix these poses improperly, you get unwanted stretching of the face.

A more solid method for mimicking realistic jaw movement is to create a skeletal jaw. Create a bone that is a child of the head bone. Then use a skinning tool to allow this bone to deform the lower part of the face. This makes it much easier to animate lateral movement of the jaw. If you want, you can also create a set of sliders: one to move the jaw up and down, another to move it left and right.

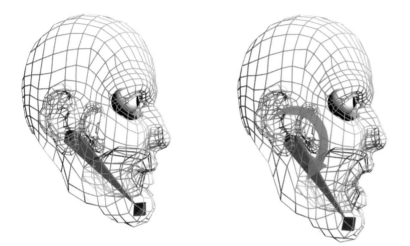

A simple jawbone enables you to open the jaw and move it from side to side with less chance of distortion.

Preset Facial Poses

When you animate the face, you are likely to find yourself always going back to a handful of standard facial poses. The most obvious are the poses used for lip-sync. Perhaps your character is a bit dimwitted and is always getting confused and twisting up his face as he thinks.

Many people simply sculpt these poses, snapshot them, and add them to the list of morph targets. This is not a good idea for several reasons. First, the more sliders you get, the more difficult it becomes to manage the animation process. Second, these additional targets add to the original muscle targets, creating a slightly unpredictable action for the sliders when they are used in combination. In the jaw movement example, having multiple sliders that affect the jaw can cause anomalous results. This is not the way to animate efficiently. The facial muscles are your primitives for *all* facial poses. It is best to keep them as the only things that directly deform the face. Any "stock" poses need to be created above this layer.

One way to create stock poses outside the normal muscle poses involves a little bit of scripting. Create a script that moves the muscle sliders to the proper position automatically. This way, you keep the number of targets as simple as possible.

1. Open the script window.

2. Dial in your pose, being sure to move every slider.

3. Drag the script to the toolbar to create a button.

4. Press the button to create the pose.

In a package such as Maya or 3ds max, you can create the scripts and place them on a custom toolbar. Pressing the button for "confusion" moves the appropriate sliders to their designated positions. From that point, you can either lock in the pose as a keyframe or tweak the sliders to get the right expression.

Replacement Animation

Mouths for this character are animated using replacement animation.

I must admit, I am a big fan of replacement animation. It can give a project a real stop-motion feel. In addition, it affords you wide latitude in modeling choices. If you're replacing mouth shapes, for example, you will not be constrained by the number of vertices in a model as you would when morphing the mouth shapes. Of course, it was used on *South Park*, which has very simple characters, but replacement animation can be used in much more complex shots.

If you understand how to create simple expressions and sliders, you can set up replacement animation without much difficulty. All it really takes is two things: visibility and an if/then statement.

Visibility

Visibility is an attribute supported by most 3D applications. As its name implies, it makes an object visible or invisible, depending on how the attribute is set. In every 3D package I've seen, if visibility is set to 0, the object is invisible and does not render. Setting visibility to 1 makes the object visible. Of course, check your software's documentation to make sure this is the case for your particular application.

If/Then

An if/then, or conditional, statement is supported in most packages that support expressions and scripting. An if/then statement usually reads something like this:

```
IF (VARIABLE = 1 )     THEN do_something
                       ELSE do_something_else
```

This generic if/then statement's syntax may take a slightly different form, depending on the software. The principle, however, is identical.

Setting Up Replacement Animation

In a replacement animation scenario, the if/then statement is tied to the position of a slider, which can be either an object in the scene or a virtual slider that shows up in a control panel.

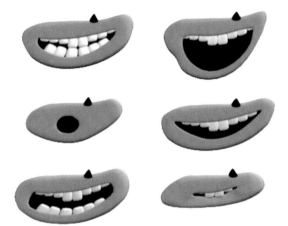

Here are a bunch of mouth shapes in a scene that can be used for replacement animation.

Say, for example, that the first mouth should appear when the slider is between 0 and 1. This can be accomplished with a simple expression on the object as follows:

```
If ((slider > 0) && (slider <=1))     then visibility=1;
                                      else visibility=0
```

In this particular expression, the symbol ">" means "greater than," the symbol "&&" means "AND," and the symbol "<=" means "less than or equal to." The parentheses are there just to keep things grouped properly.

If you want to translate all this into plain English, you can say that if the value of the slider is "greater than" 0 "and" the value of slider is "less than or equal to" 1, then set the visibility of the object to 1. Otherwise, set the visibility to 0.

When the slider is between 0 and 1, the object is visible. By moving the slider, you can turn the object on and off.

Once you get one object working, the rest is easy. Simply increment the number in the if/then statement and apply it to the other objects, as follows:

```
If ((slider > 1) && (slider <=2))  then visibility=1;
                                    else visibility=0
If ((slider > 2) && (slider <=3))  then visibility=1;
                                    else visibility=0
```

… and so on.

Set up the rest of the mouths so that as the slider increments, each mouth's visibility toggles on and off.

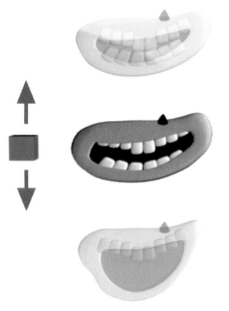

Keep in mind that the slider controlling the visibility must "jump" from value to value using a step controller or curve rather than move linearly or along a curve. This prevents unwanted objects from being revealed as the slider moves from value to value.

Set-Driven Keys and Replacement Animation

If expressions frighten you, then you can always set up replacement animation using set-driven keys. For each mouth shape, create set-driven keys that are controlled by the slider. The first mouth will then turn on at 0, off at 1; the second mouth on at 1, off at 2, and so on. The resulting curves look like step curves.

Skinning

Once you have a good skeleton, you can use it to deform the character's skin. Skinning tools have taken great strides in the past few years, and it is very easy to create a character that deforms the way you want it to.

Deformers

Many packages have introduced the concept of *joint deformers* to help with the skinning process. These usually take the form of lattices that surround a character's joint. By sculpting the lattice or manipulating a control panel that modifies the lattice, you can fine-tune the deformation as the joint bends. Joint deformers can help considerably with a number of problems.

Another type of deformer is called a *morph deformer*. It gives you great latitude in that it allows you to literally sculpt a deformation as a morph target, exactly matching the outline of the skin based upon the angle of the joint.

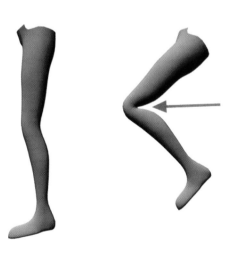

Without any additional control, most packages deform a cylindrical shape, such as a knee or an elbow.

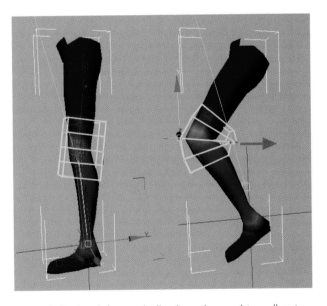

A simple lattice deformer (yellow) can be used to pull out the back of the knee as the joint bends.

Knees and Elbows

One of the most common deformation problems is that the backs of the knees and elbows flatten unnaturally as the joint bends. A simple lattice deformer can help tremendously in keeping the profile of the joint natural.

The result is a more natural profile.

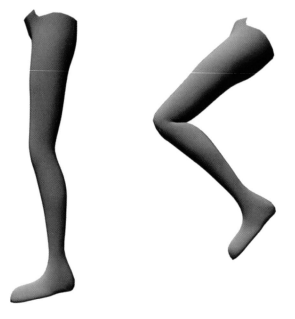

Shoulders

Shoulders can be a big problem. If you don't want to create a realistic shoulder blade setup, you can get much of the same effect using a morph deformer. This changes the shape of the back based upon the angle of the shoulder.

Conclusion

That should give you a basic understanding of what's involved in rigging a character. These tips and techniques should get you through most basic characters, but there are always exceptions and times where you need to create a new and novel solution. When rigging a character, always keep in mind that the ultimate goal is to animate the thing.

Animation Tips & Tricks

When you think about it, animation is nothing more than a series of tricks. Each trick is designed to fool the audience into thinking the characters are actually alive. Over the years, animators have developed a fairly large bag of tricks.

This chapter goes over many of these tricks and techniques. Many of these hail from classic animators going back to Disney. Others are more recent and are geared toward 3D animation. When animating for the audience, use whatever tricks you need to make your characters come to life.

Making Characters Think

The main goal of the animator is to bring the character to life. To do this, the character needs to think. Thoughts drive the way a character moves. Don't animate just motions. Animate ideas, thoughts, and emotions. Doing so guides the way your character moves and interacts with others.

Always ask yourself, "What is this character thinking?" It is the character's thoughts and emotions that move the body. They give meaning to the character's motions. A character driving a car has no meaning; a man driving his pregnant wife to the hospital has meaning.

Thinking Starts in the Head

The brain is where thinking happens. A thinking character has an operating brain, which sends electrical signals to the rest of the body. Whatever happens with the body, it all starts in the head.

One simple trick many animators use is to lead motions with the head. If a character has eyes, the eyes start moving first, then the head, and finally the body. How much the eyes lead the body depends on the situation. The character's thoughts must be clear to the audience before the motion happens. A character has an evil thought, and then turns to an unsuspecting victim. A character sees that he's won the lottery, and then jumps for joy.

Characters Are Whole

In this book, as well as many others on animation, the body tends to get broken down into parts. One section tells you how to animate the hands, another focuses on the face, and so on. This is necessary when you are learning, but when you get into animation, you must pull all these parts together and animate the character as a whole.

Pose and animate the entire character, not just individual parts. A slight change to one part of the body may affect others. If a hand gesture is not working, for example, the problem may not be in the hand, but the body. Be sure to step back from the process and look at the whole character. Many times your first idea is not the best for posing. If the pose is not working, don't be afraid to start from scratch.

50/50 Rule

Typically, 50% of animation is preparation; the other 50% is actual animation. You need to fully understand the character and the scene before setting hand to mouse. Master Disney animators would make pages of sketches to work out poses for a simple action.

Preparation is also experimentation. You need to explore all the possibilities of a scene as you prepare to animate it. In many cases, your first instinct is the most obvious choice—what the audience expects. Going on first instincts may shut off many avenues that can be much more fruitful in the long run.

Simplicity Is Key

One thing that cannot be stressed too much is the importance of keeping things simple. Try to come up with the simplest and most direct poses and motions that you can for your characters. Too much motion will simply spoil the action and confuse the audience. Simplicity is always much more readable to an audience than complexity.

Dialogue

Dialogue animation is always depicted as one of the more difficult skills to master. This is not entirely true. If you want a difficult task, try communicating the same information contained within a line of dialogue with body postures alone—it's like trying to ask for the restroom in a country where you don't know the language.

Dialogue communicates volumes of information to the audience. It also gives the animator a lot to use when creating a scene. The dialogue has an emotional content and tone of voice, as well as a distinct rhythm that the animator can use for timing. After reading the track, the animator should know exactly what parts of the dialogue to emphasize during the scene.

Listening to the Track

Before you animate anything, you need to first listen to the dialogue track intently. Listen to the track several times until you have it memorized. As you listen, close your eyes and try to mentally picture yourself as the character. Pretty soon, you will get an idea as to what the character needs to be doing as the dialogue is spoken. This is where acting really enters the picture. You need to place yourself in the character's frame of mind to understand how the character will act. This process gives you the poses.

As you listen, you get a sense as to the rhythm of the track as well. Certain words are emphasized more than others. Make a note of this on your script, because these are the major beats of the dialogue. Typically, your character's major gestures happen near the beats. This process gives you the timing. After you have the poses and the timing, you can begin to block out the animation.

The Body and Dialogue

In long shots, the body is much more visible than the face. Getting the body to sync with the dialogue can sometimes be more important than getting the lips to sync. Imagine two snippets of animation. In both, the character is saying the same line of dialogue. The first one animates just the face; the second animates just the body. Which character do you think would appear more alive?

If just the face is animated, the character appears lifeless.

If just the body is animated, the character looks more alive.

As you can see from just the still images, the animation using the body alone looks much more dynamic and realistic. It also shows how important body motions are in communication. The only exception would be in those shots where the character's body is not visible: the close-up shot. If your posing and animation already describe the dialogue to the audience, then the actual facial lip sync is simply the frosting on the cake to emphasize the mood and words.

Exercise #1: Animating Dialogue

Take a simple line of dialogue and create two animations. In the first, just the mouth moves. In the second, just the body moves.

The Body Anticipates Dialogue

For some reason, the motion of the body anticipates the actual dialogue by a few frames. The unspoken thought seems to manifest itself in the motions of the hands and body before the thought is voiced. Think of a character who's having a difficult time saying something—perhaps a confession of love. As he searches for the right thing to say, his hands gesture the thought several seconds before he spits the words out. This is true even in normal conversation.

...know   ...a   ....b - i l l - ion

The motion of the body anticipates dialogue by a few frames.

Lift the Head Before Dialogue Begins

In a similar vein, when a character starts speaking, the head and body lift both physically and in attitude 4-6 frames before the mouth starts talking. This happens partly because the character needs to take a breath before talking, but more importantly, the character needs to think about what to say.

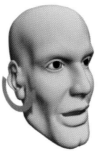

Lift the head before a character speaks dialogue.

Break the Dialogue into Phrases

When animating the body, try to break the dialogue into phrases. Each phrase should have one major action. Think of Robert DeNiro in *Taxi Driver* when he says

> Are you talking to me?
>
> Are YOU…
>
> …talking to ME?

This dialogue has natural pauses that break it up into three natural phrases. These phrases bracket the motions of the character. Each phrase has one major motion.

The Mouth and Dialogue

The mouth is very important to dialogue. If the lips are generally in sync, the audience accepts the character. If the lips are out of sync, then the audience senses something is wrong. Lips that are overanimated also stand out like a sore thumb.

Simplify the Mouths

The best way to get smooth mouth motion is to concentrate on phrases rather than individual phonemes. An extreme example is rapid dialogue. In this case, the phonemes occur more frequently than once per frame. Animating even at one phoneme per frame makes the character's mouth appear to strobe or stutter. Typically, you should keep most mouth poses on the screen for at least two frames so that they are readable.

With this in mind, be sure to hit the mouth accent on the vowel. Vowels are always the loudest sounds, as well as the longest. When animating a vowel, open the mouth quickly—within two frames—and close it slowly for as many frames as the vowel lasts.

When animating vowels, pop the mouth open quickly and close it slowly.

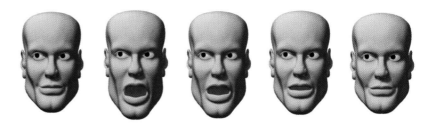

Use Overlap

One of the most common mistakes in animating the mouth is to quickly create the phoneme shapes and let the computer do the in-betweens. This winds up looking incredibly mechanical. Just like motions of the body; motions in the face need to overlap.

If you're animating your mouth shapes using muscle-based morph targets, then you can adjust the curves slightly so that the motions overlap by a frame or two. This smoothes out the mouth motion, so that the resulting animation looks more natural.

Varying Phonemes

Another mistake is using a single set of stock phoneme shapes for all of a character's lip sync. This will give the audience no variety in the mouth shapes, which will make the character look mechanical.

As with overlap, muscle-based morph targets can help a lot. Go back over the animation and mix up the curves. If the character has a loud vowel sound, open the jaw more. Add some asymmetry by turning up the smile on one side of the face. In general, do whatever it takes to make the mouth match the character of the dialogue track on any given frame.

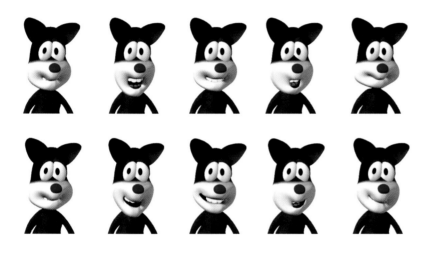

This dialogue animation uses stock mouth shapes.

By varying the shapes of the mouths, you make the character look more lifelike.

Teeth

When animating the mouth, be careful not to expose too much of the teeth. Women usually show upper teeth only when talking. Men show either upper or lower teeth, but rarely both. People show both sets of teeth only in extreme situations, such as when screaming or afraid. If you animate your characters so that both sets of teeth are visible in a normal situation, the audience interprets it as abnormal.

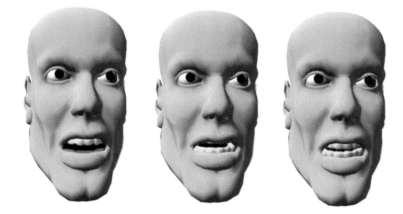

Characters usually show the top or bottom teeth, but rarely both.

Facial Animation

Facial animation is closely associated with dialogue, but many facial animation tricks fall outside the area of lip sync. A character's face needs to be able to react without having to speak. Changes in facial expression are a big part of reacting.

Expression Changes

When the face undergoes a significant change of expression, the audience's point of interest needs to be the face. In these situations, you need to pose the character so that the face is clearly visible to the audience. Keep the character in that pose when the expression changes. If the body moves too much, its motion overwhelms the action of the face. If the head moves too much, the audience cannot see the face at all. Psychological gestures can be very poignant in these subtle changes in expression.

Eyes

The classic saying "the eyes are the mirror of the soul" is based to a large degree in fact. The eyes really do tell the audience a great deal about what the character is thinking and feeling. Many times, the eyes tell the audience more than the dialogue.

Making Eye Contact

The most important aspect of animating the eyes is keeping eye contact focused on the object of interest. If the character's eyes appear to be looking elsewhere, it looks like it is distracted or spaced out.

Eye contact is a tricky thing, however. The next time you're in a conversation, try to notice how often you make eye contact. Usually, it is only a fraction of the time. In fact, if someone stares at you constantly while talking, it appears abnormal.

Character has his eyes on the ball. Even a slight change in eye direction is noticeable to the audience.

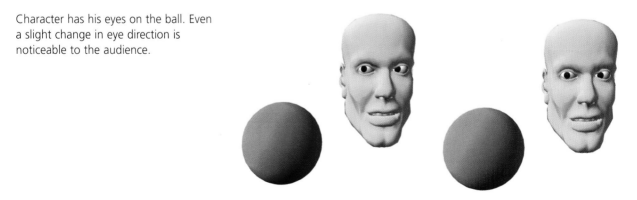

Breaking eye contact is as important as making it. If a character becomes embarrassed or evasive, it tends to look away. Confident people usually make more frequent eye contact when talking to others. Nervous and surprised people can be wide-eyed, whereas untrustworthy and defensive people often squint and dart their eyes from left to right.

Psychologists have discovered that infants are very sensitive to eye direction, so some of this awareness may be hardwired into our brains. Among social species, eye direction indicates where another individual is looking and what that individual's future actions might be.

Eye Direction and Thought

There is a whole area of research that maps what people think to the directions their eyes move. Psychologists, among others, use this information to find visual cues to how people think. Try remembering what you had for breakfast without moving your eyes. You can't do it. Each thought that goes through a person's head triggers an unconscious motion in the eyes. These motions can actually be mapped and used to the animator's advantage.

Typically, eye motions to the left mean the character is remembering something. Eye motion to the right means the character is constructing something new. This may mean he's thinking out a problem, or it could also be that he is fabricating a lie, or it may mean the character is simply confused or guessing.

The level of the eye also plays a role in the thought process. Eyes looking up indicate visual thoughts. A character looking up and left is remembering an image. Looking up and to the right means he is constructing an image.

The middle levels are associated with sound. Eyes looking directly left mean a character is remembering something that was said. Looking right would mean he is constructing a new sentence.

The lower levels deal with emotion. Eyes looking diagonally down left indicate an internal dialogue. Feelings and emotions are expressed when a person looks down diagonally right.

Lids

The most common thing that lids are used for is blinking. Characters should blink every once in a while just so that they look alive. Blinks can also be used to great effect to draw attention to the character's face, such as in a change of eye direction.

When animating lids, the first instinct is to keep the lids fully open so that the character seems alert. If you keep the lids 100% open, however, then you can't open them wider, such as when the character is shocked or surprised. It is better to keep the "normal" lid of the character somewhere around 80% open instead. This keeps the character alert, but in a relaxed way. Plus, it gives you some flexibility for opening the eyes wider.

Warm personalities open the eyes wider, which can also be a sign of intelligence or attentive listening. These open communicators make use of smiling eye. In the most extreme cases, a smiling cheek lifts so high, it affects the lower outline of the eye, pushing it up into a crescent, or "smiling eye." In contrast, an angry person may stare with squinted eyes for an uncomfortable length of time. It has recently been discovered that people close their eyes briefly before giving a false answer.

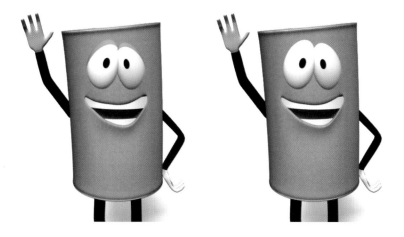

The lids should usually be kept slightly relaxed so that they can open wider.

Pupils

Dilation of the pupils is one area that is often overlooked when animating a character. In a realistic scene, eye dilation from moment to moment is usually very subtle, but it can go a long way to indicate mood. Think of the scene in *Jurassic Park* where the T-Rex looks in the window of the car and the eye dilates when the flashlight hits it. The motion of the eye itself is what kept the character from appearing to be a giant puppet. This is an extreme example, and the size of the pupil usually remains fairly constant within a scene, changing between scenes as the character's mood and environment change.

Typically, the bigger the pupil, the more innocent and childlike a character seems. A character with small pupils seems to have "beady eyes" and appears to be less trustworthy. The quality of light in the scene also affects the pupils. More light results in smaller pupils; less light results in bigger pupils. If a character is dying of thirst in a sun-parched desert, make sure his pupils match the situation.

Animating the Body

As you saw in the in the earlier section on dialogue, the body can communicate a great deal of information to the audience. In addition to dialogue, the body is incredibly important to any animation. Here are some tips and tricks for animating the body.

Overcoming Stiffness

When animation is critiqued, the most frequently heard comment is that a character looks "stiff." This usually happens when a character's motions are not overlapped and do not flow smoothly. Not all parts of the body move at the same time. This has been talked about before as the concepts of overlap and follow-through.

Don't Stop

The first rule of thumb is to never let your characters come to a full stop. If they are alive, they are moving in one way or another. It may be a simple blink or a slight shifting of weight, but every motion of a character flows into another motion.

Successive Bending of Joints

Another way to overcome stiffness is to adhere to the principle of "successive bending of joints," also known as "successive breaking of joints." This means that as a character's motions overlap, each joint bends successively. You can compare it to a whip-like motion where the base moves, then the middle section, and then the end. Imagine an arm reaching out to grab something. The base or upper arm comes to extension first, followed by the lower arm, and then slightly later by the hand. If you offset keyframes rather than give each part of the arm the same timing, the motion is more fluid and natural-looking.

Successive bending of joints means that as a character's motions overlap; each joint bends successively.

Snap

Snap is action that happens faster than the eye can see. In film terms, it's action that happens in less than a frame, and it's the kind of timing that is most associated with "good timing." If you watch your fingers as you snap them, it's almost impossible to see the fingers in mid-snap. The most you might see is a blur between the snap positions.

The best way to add snap in animation is to mix slow and quick motions and a good dose of overshoot. The contrast of slow and fast gives the quick moves the most snap. Start with a nice moving hold. Anticipate the new motion so the audience knows it's coming. As you animate the new motion, follow through quickly to the extreme position. Try to put one wild overshoot position the frame before the actual extreme position. Make the overshoot fairly exaggerated. Because it is so quick, the overshoot doesn't need to be anatomically correct; it is there just to add snap.

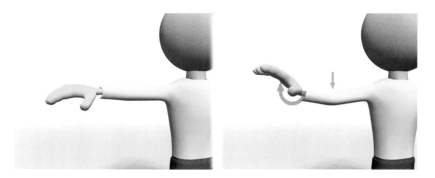

To get more snap, insert a wild overshoot position before the extreme.

Hand and Arm Motion

Try bending your wrist up and down without moving your forearm. It's pretty much impossible. When the wrist goes up, the forearm naturally moves down slightly, and vice versa. This happens because the muscles that move the palm of the hand at the wrist are located in the forearm. In addition, many of the muscles that move the fingers are also located in the forearm.

When the wrist bends up, the action of muscles within the forearm cause the forearm to angle down.

Conversely, when the wrist bends down, the forearm naturally moves up for the same reason.

When the wrist twists, the radius and ulna within the forearm rotate about one another.

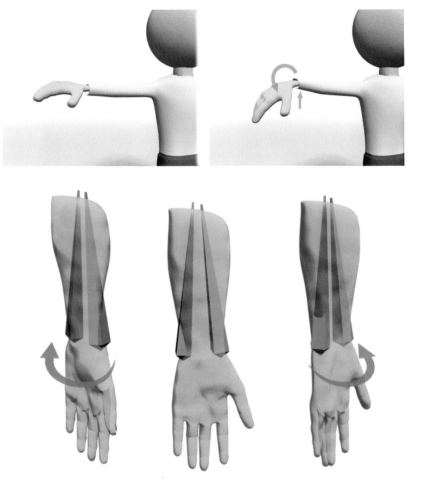

In most cases, the motion of the arms drives the motion of the hands. Hand motion actually begins in the forearm. This causes the hand to move slightly later than the arm. (This is very much like successive bending of joints.) In addition to muscle action, the hands also drag behind the arm in broad motions because of secondary motion, in the same way that a dog's floppy ears drag behind the motion of the head.

When animating hands, be sure to recognize that the motion of a relaxed hand always follows that of the arm.

Of course, there are those exceptions when secondary motion is much less prevalent, such as when the hand is tense for one reason or another. The hand is perfectly stiff during a karate chop, for example. If a character is holding a hot bowl of soup, the rest of the body moves so that the hands can remain relatively still with relation to the soup.

Secondary motion and hands.

Grabbing/Gripping

I've always found it interesting that real people pick up and hold things without thought, but getting a virtual character to do the same can be a big problem.

If the object is stable, such as a handrail, then IK must be used on the arms. This allows the wrist and hand to remain stationary as the rest of the character moves. If the object is being held, as with a coffee cup, then either IK or FK can be used on the arms.

Constraints

If a character grabs and then subsequently lets go of an object, you probably need to use a constraint. A position constraint causes an object to follow the position of another object. Some packages also support weighted constraints, which constrain the object to the average position of several objects. Once the constraint is assigned, the object becomes fixed to the target object's position. Animating the target's position causes the constrained object to follow.

If the character is holding a coffee cup, then you place a constraint on the cup, fixing it to the hand that is holding it. If the character sets down the cup, then the constraint is released, or its weight is animated to zero. If the character switches the cup to another hand, then the weight is shifted to the opposite hand or a second constraint added.

Takes and Double Takes

One of the more fun parts of animation is when you have a chance to do a cartoon "take." A take is your character's reaction to something unexpected. How you do the take depends wholly on your character and the situation. It can be wild, wacky, and completely over the top, as in a classic cartoon, or more subtle. Sometimes a small and subtle reaction has a much better effect than a reaction that's extremely exaggerated. Realistic characters don't usually go into bug-eyed hysterics, for example. There are no rules, however, and wild takes can be very effective, particularly at times when you need maximum contrast.

There are two broad categories of takes: a normal take and a double take. In the normal take, the character reacts almost immediately. If his hand gets whacked with a mallet, for instance, the reaction would probably be immediate, hence the take. In a double take, the reaction takes a while to set in, and the audience can see the transformation as the character realizes what has happened. Someone giving your character a check for a million dollars is a great setup for a double take. It takes a while to realize just how much money that is. Once the news sets in, however, the reaction can be huge.

How do you actually animate a take? Some of that depends on the type of take you're animating. Look at a typical wild take to see what it's made of.

The take is a few simple poses timed for maximum impact. First, you have an anticipation, where the head squashes down before going into the take. A huge action such as a take demands quite a bit of overshoot, so you probably need another pose at that point. Finally, you have the take itself.

In a take, start with a normal pose.

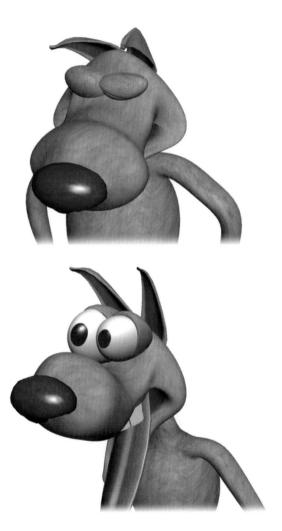

The head then squashes into the shoulders, anticipating the take.

Finally, the head rises up into the take, overshooting the final position before settling in.

The timing of a take really depends on the action. In the double take, the slow realization can be milked for up to several seconds. For the take itself, there will be an anticipation before the take of anywhere from 4 to 20 frames—the more violent the take, the bigger the anticipation. After that, the character goes into his take, overshooting the final pose by a few frames. Once the character is into the take itself, you might want to vibrate the head and facial features a bit to keep them looking alive. Even after the take, you may want to make your character collapse into a quivering glob of jelly.

Be aware that a take is simply a reaction, and the size of the take is directly proportional to the situation. A small reaction needs only a small take—as small as a simple blink. Your character does not need to go into jaw-dropping, eye-popping takes at every twist and turn of the plot. Instead, save the big take for the big moment. When it happens, the take is that much stronger.

You don't need a face with bulging eyes to do a take. This faceless little vacuum does a nice, simple take in reaction to the hose.

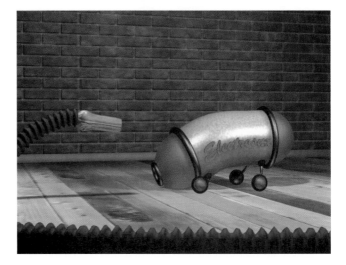

Staggers

What happens when your character is hit on the head, stretched to the point of breaking, or riding along a bumpy road? In each of these situations, you might want your character's motion to vibrate or stutter. To get this type of motion, you need to use a stagger.

A stagger is a timing and positioning effect. You move the object back and forth between staggered points—generally taking two steps forward for every one back. If you have points A, B, C, and D in a line, the object moves from A past B to C, then back to B then on past C to D, then back to C and so on. This gives the object a less linear movement, producing a stuttering effect. This same type of motion can be cycled as well, for something like a character's head ringing like a bell. When doing such effects, strobing can be a serious problem. A liberal dose of motion blur covers this strobing quite well, however.

You can also play with the spacing of the stagger to enhance or diminish its effect. For a deeper stutter, animate three steps forward for every two steps back. For a more subtle effect, animate five steps forward for every one step back.

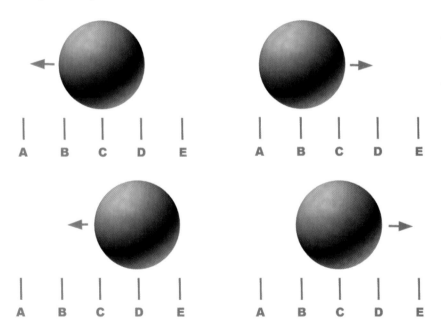

A stagger is a back-and-forth motion—taking two steps forward, then one back, for example. This simple stagger goes from A to C, back to B, forward to D, back to C, forward to E, and so on.

The same principle applies to rotations, as in this vibrating head. The positions in this animation are A C B D B C A. The resulting animation can then be cycled. This type of motion can strobe very easily, so a good dose of motion blur helps to smooth things out.

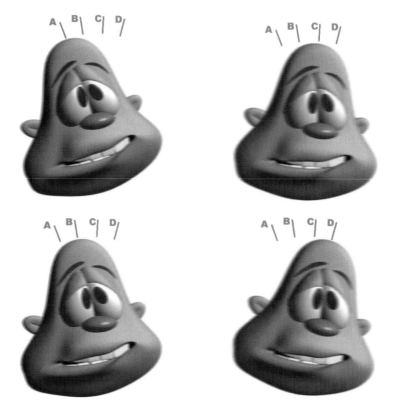

Animating Laughter

When animating laughter, you first must realize it is an action that involves the entire body. The head, shoulders, chest, and belly all play a role in creating a laugh. There are as many laughs as there are personalities, but here are a few generalizations to help guide you.

To laugh, you usually take a deep breath followed by a series of short exhales. The deep breath pushes the shoulders and head back, which come forward again during the laugh. When laughing, the head and shoulders bounce up and down along with the contracting belly, which on heavy characters can jiggle quite a bit. As the head moves forward, staggering the timing of poses can make the laugh a bit more realistic.

Breakdown of a Laugh

The absolute guide for timing the laugh is the dialogue track. Each laugh has a unique rhythm, which you can usually notice quite easily if the track is read properly. Making sure your character's laugh is in sync with the track helps you to pull off the shot.

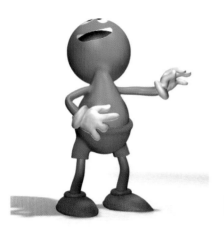

When laughing, your character should throw his head back as he takes a deep breath.

He then exhales as he laughs, his head bobbing up and down…

…and up again as the head moves forward.

This should all happen in time with the dialogue track for the duration of the laugh.

Multiple Characters

Most films have more than one character. Animating multiple characters in a scene does not have to be a difficult problem. It's just a matter of breaking the problem down into manageable chunks and proceeding from there. When you work with groups, many times you have to create an animated version of "hot potato," with the focus of the scene shifting from one character to another.

Choreography

The interactions of characters in a scene follow a certain kind of choreography. Just like actors, animated characters need to "hit their mark" so that the scene flows smoothly. When you block out a scene, try to keep the compositions interesting. Use staging to create contrast between characters.

Who Comes First

When approaching a shot with multiple characters, you need to decide where to start. It is a good idea to animate the dominant character first. This is the character who is talking, leading, threatening, or otherwise driving the action of the shot. Because the other characters react to the dominant character, they need something to guide their reactions.

In a situation where the emphasis shifts from character to character, you may have to approach the scene in stages. My suggestion is to block out the basic scene so that you understand the broad choreography, and then work through the scene with all characters speaking a line of dialogue at a time. Animate the first character speaking, then the reactions of the other characters, then animate the next line of dialogue using the next character, and so on.

Crowds

The sticky subject of crowd animation gets into some of the more challenging aspects of 3D. For large crowds, many companies use custom software that works more like particle systems, directing the flow of characters across the scene. Each character is given a handful of generic motions to perform, and the crowd-generation software directs these motions.

When animating crowds, think of the crowd as more of a mass that can be used to highlight the main action. Contrast is also very important. If the main character is moving around a lot, keep the crowd still so that the main character pops against the crowd. Conversely, a very still character also pops against an active crowd.

Environment

Finally, when your character exists solely on a computer, it is very easy to forget that it is supposed to be in a virtual world and needs to interact with it. The world your characters inhabit has a definite effect on them. Characters behave much differently depending on where they are. The most obvious example is that a character in outer space is weight-less, whereas one on the earth is not. The force of gravity is absent to the astronaut in space.

Other environmental forces also affect your character. If the sun is really bright, a character may squint its eyes unconsciously. If it is cold outside, the character is likely to hold its limbs close to the body to keep warm. A character walking in snow walks much differently than one walking at the beach. A character walking into the wind leans into the walk to counteract the force of the wind.

Conclusion

When animating, be sure to always put your character first. Don't let your desire to animate a really nifty motion get in the way of what the character would actually do. Stay true to your characters, making sure to keep them honest to what they would do in the world.

Keep your animation simple and direct. Try to animate one motion and emotion at a time. Remember that the mind is the pilot for all action. At any given frame, the character has one thought and emotion going through its head. Illustrate that one thought on that one frame.

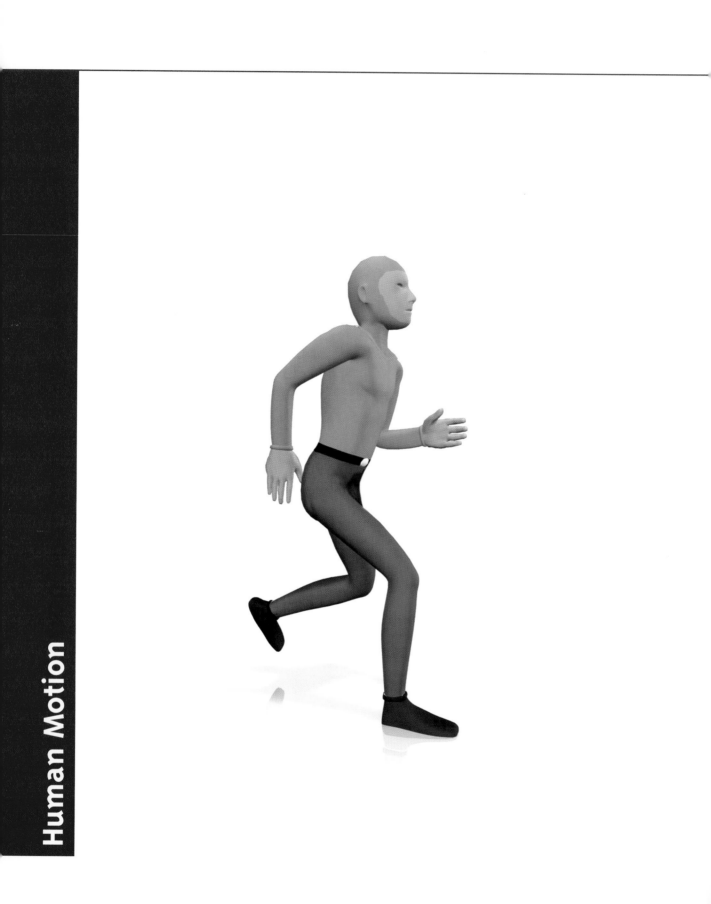

CHAPTER 5

Human Motion

The body is a complex system of joints and muscles. Understanding how it moves requires a thorough understanding of the system and a little bit about the physics of force and motion. The best way for any animator to truly understand how to move a body naturally is to use the powers of observation. Being able to look at a particular motion and understand why every part of the body is moving gives you a much better foundation for creating motion from scratch. No matter how complex the motion, it can be broken down into its constituent parts.

Using Reference

One of the best ways to understand how the body moves is to observe it in action. Good reference helps immensely when you need to break down a particular motion. If you have a video camera, you can tape yourself or a friend as reference. If you need to animate sports moves, taping this week's game should give you lots of reference. If you need to animate dance moves, perhaps rent a movie musical with lots of dancing.

Another source of reference is motion capture files. Now I know this is a bad word in some circles, but being able to watch and scrub a particular character move in 3D can be excellent reference. Remember, however, it is reference only and should be treated just as you would a videotape of a motion. Most motion capture is rather generic and does not have the nuances associated with a particular character. Keyframing the character yourself gives you much more control, quality, and character than motion capture.

Although reference is good, don't take it literally. Reference is simply meant to give you a feel for the move. You still need to re-create the move as a particular character would. Although he or she may use the same basic steps, a ballet move by a professional dancer will be a lot different from a ballet move by a professional comedian.

Being able to analyze reference motion is a great way to improve both your observation powers and your understanding of how the human body moves. Being able to break down a motion into its constituent parts is a skill any animator should develop.

Balance and Weight

One of the most important keys to creating good animation is a good understanding of balance and weight. This involves a bit of physics as well. The body is a system with a handful of major components: legs, hips, spine, shoulders, and arms. Typically, the system remains in balance, usually against the force of gravity, but also against any number of other forces. Moving any one part of the body throws the entire system out of balance. This causes the other parts of the body to reposition themselves in order to maintain balance in the system.

Another way to truly understand balance is to study line drawing. I know a lot of computer artists who don't like drawing, but even quick studies in gesture or 30-second sketches are instrumental in finding the line of action and understanding basic concepts, such as balance, weight, and transference of force. Learning the ability to create a quick sketch of a pose will help your animation immensely.

Gravity and Other Forces

In most animation, your characters need to interact with the rest of the world. This usually involves having your character react to a force of some form or another. Gravity plays a big part in creating forces. A character lifting a heavy object, for instance, is working against gravity. Many other forces also play a role. Water skiers, for example, use the force of the towrope to pull them along. A character involved in a fight may experience the force of a blow. The wind, water, and many other natural phenomena also interact with the character.

Because forces can come from so many different places and directions, it's best to look at the commonalties of forces and how they affect the body. Forces generally have three major components: strength, direction, and point of application. From these three bits of information, you can pretty much determine how the body is going to react.

A character lifting a big suitcase experiences a force at the hand, pulling straight down under the force of gravity. The size of the force is determined by the mass of the suitcase: the bigger the suitcase, the more force. As this force pulls down on the hand, the shoulder and spine bend in the direction of the force. The lower body also gets into the act, causing the leg to stiffen on the side of the body where the force is acting.

A heavy suitcase exerts a force straight down, pulling the arm down and twisting the spine to the side.

When the character moves in this manner, it is actually using the force of its muscles to oppose that of gravity and the suitcase. This is where balance enters into the equation. To keep the suitcase at a constant level, the force from the character's muscles must balance that of suitcase. If the character applies too little force, the suitcase wins. Too much force, and the character topples over in the opposite direction.

A character tripping on a curb experiences a force directed from the curb and applied to the foot. The strength of the force is determined by the speed of the character. In addition to this, there is also the force of the momentum, which carries the body forward. This causes the character to pivot forward at the toe.

Character Mass

Another force to consider is the weight of the character itself. Lack of "weight" is one of the most common errors found in animation. Every character has mass and weight, which affect the way it moves. Just like with the suitcase, a character needs to balance the weight of its own body against the force of gravity.

The relative mass of a character is also very important. A heavy character stands differently and moves differently than a lighter character for the simple reason that the heavy character has more weight to move around. The extra weight causes the character to bend its knees more as it stands. A big belly also affects posture by pulling the spine forward and

Both of these characters are the same height, but the extra mass in the heavier character makes its knees bend a bit more. The extra weight in the belly also pulls the spine forward, forcing the shoulders back.

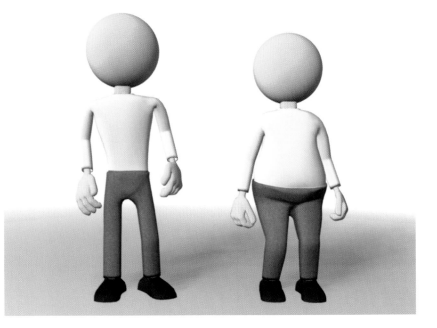

forcing the character's shoulders back to compensate. A pregnant woman is a good example of this effect. Extra weight also causes the character to exert more energy during such tasks as walking and running.

How the Body Moves

Once you understand how the body maintains balance and how forces affect the body, you can begin to understand how the body interacts with itself to create motion. A body can use the force of its own muscles to throw itself out of balance, causing it to move.

Muscle Energy

Muscles store and release energy. Typically, the more a limb is bent, the more energy it stores. This is because a fully bent joint pulls the muscles much like a rubber band, storing energy and giving the muscles maximum distance with which to pull the joint. The longer the muscles pull, the more energy is transferred to the limb. In a jump, for example, the more the knee is bent, the higher the jump. In animation, this is directly related to squash and stretch. A character that is squashed has more energy than one that is stretched.

This bent arm is storing energy in the tricep. The more it is bent, the longer the tricep can pull, and the more energy it can exert.

Who will jump higher? The more a joint bends, the more muscle energy it stores.

Pendulum Effect

Because of the pendulum effect, limbs can swing much like pendulums as the body moves. An arm performs this motion in a walk, swinging forward and back. This is natural in a lot of motions, and many times the arms or the legs move in this manner. The pendulum effect of arms is specifically part of the body counter-balancing itself. It is an unconscious motion that is an integral part of motion, not secondary motion.

In a walk, the arms move like a pendulum.

A baseball pitcher extends his arm fully to allow the hand and ball to traverse the maximum distance to gain maximum velocity.

The pendulum effect can also be a way for bodies to transmit and direct energy. A long pendulum traveling at the same rotational speed has more energy than a short one, because the longer pendulum has to travel more distance per rotation. In a similar way, extending an arm or a leg outward like a pendulum makes it possible for the corresponding foot or hand to travel faster. A baseball pitcher, for example, extends his arm fully as the pitch is thrown. This allows the hand and ball to traverse the maximum distance to gain maximum velocity.

Another example might be a child on a swing. The child extends the legs on the forward swing to gain energy and swing higher. On the swing back, the child bends the knees and tucks the legs close to the body to conserve energy. This way, each forward swing adds energy to the system, so that the child can swing higher. If the child kept the legs straight on the back swing, the energy gained on the forward swing would be lost.

Spinning

One interesting effect that seems counterintuitive is what happens when a character twists or spins. Usually, when a character pulls the arms into the body, the rotational velocity increases. A diver doing a flip tucks the legs in to achieve maximum spin. An ice skater spins faster when the arms move into the body. This compression also functions to compress the center of gravity to focus and conserve energy while reducing drag.

Some people may think that having the arms or legs close to the body is what creates the energy. Tucking the limbs simply transfers energy gained elsewhere. Close examination shows that these types of motions all start with extended limbs. The diver throws the arms above the head to get maximum energy. As the arms move down like a pendulum, the body curls up into a tuck, pulling the newly gained energy from the arms toward the center of the body and causing it to spin. The ice skater spins with the arms outstretched first to gain energy, then pulls the arms in, spinning faster as energy is transferred closer to and center of rotation. Conversely, throwing arms or legs outward after the motion has been started slows down rotation.

Animating Locomotion

Now that you understand some of the basics of motion, you can now apply it to more complex motion. If you look at any motion, no matter how complex, you can break it down into some fundamental components. These include the basic tenets of animation, such as squash and stretch, anticipation, secondary motion, and so on. On a more advanced level, you need to understand the transfer of weight and energy, as well.

Changing Speed

One of the most common motions that animators need to create are those involved with locomotion. (*Digital Character Animation 2, Volume I* already covered the basics of walks and runs.) Walking or running at a constant rate in a perfectly straight line makes for boring animation, however. It's important to analyze motion to look at ways to change such things as the speed and direction your characters travel.

Walk to Run

Because a run is a series of leaps, transitioning from a walk to a run requires that the character take a leap. This particular transition occurs over one step, but characters may also speed up the walk and transition to a run over the course of several strides.

1. Start with a standard walk.

2. As the character begins the run, the body leans forward.

3. A few frames later, the forward knee bends more as the character gets ready to leap. The shoulders rotate and the forward arm crosses in front of the chest.

4. The body straightens out as the run begins. (The first step of the run.)

Run to Walk

In transitioning from a run to a walk, a character needs to absorb the energy of the run. Typically, this cannot happen in a single step, so the character takes progressively shorter steps over a span of several strides.

1. Start with a basic run.

2. As the character takes the last step of the run, the shoulders move back and the hips pivot forward. This allows the character to direct more energy into the leg and foot.

3. As the character lands, this energy is transferred through the leg as the knee bends to absorb the shock. The arms move outward from the body to maintain balance.

4. As the energy is dissipated, the character slows down into a walk.

Changing Direction

Similar transitions may take place between any number of strides—from a walk to a skip, sneak, or tiptoe, for example. In all of these, the concepts are similar to the transition between a walk and a run in that the character is changing its momentum and pattern of footsteps. In a walk to a sneak, for example, the character would slow down the rate of footsteps and crouch the body lower.

Turns

Most walks and runs done as animation exercises are in a straight line. This looks great until your character needs to turn a corner. Turning a character is not a difficult task but does require a little bit of extra attention.

A gentle turn, usually more than four or five steps, can be accomplished by turning the feet and hips slightly on each successive step. One thing to watch is the direction of the knees. Depending on how the character is set up, it may be very easy to turn the feet without affecting the knees. Be sure to rotate the legs at the thigh to maintain the proper leg direction. If your setup has null objects to control the knees, you can use those as well.

As the body turns, the shoulders lean slightly toward the center of the turn. In a gentle turn, this is hardly noticeable, but in a running turn, it might be more of a factor.

Single-Step Turn

If the character needs to turn quickly, say in a step or two, you probably need to pivot the feet. This is a fairly easy animation task, but make sure that the foot pivots at the ball of the toe and that this point of the foot doesn't slip.

1. Start with a basic walk.

2. As the character begins to turn, the character will start to pivot on the inside toe. The head will also begin to turn.

3. The shoulders counter-rotate to maintain balance as the outside foot swings around.

4. The outside foot sets down and the shoulders start rotating back.

5. The character takes one more step and the walk continues as normal.

Running Turn

A run carries a lot more energy than a walk, so changing direction requires more effort. Just as a transition from a run to a walk may occur over several steps, the running turn may also take several steps, because the character needs to slow down before taking off in a different direction. Think of how the silent movie comedians exaggerated running turns by hopping on one foot for several steps during the turn, almost like a car skidding to a stop.

1. Start with a run. In a typical run, the upper body leans forward and the arms pump.

2. The character needs to slow before the turn. To do this, the arms stop pumping and the body leans back.

3. The body pivots on the right foot as the left foot swings forward and to the side.

4. The weight transfers to the left foot, and the body has the maximum lean into the turn. At this point, the left arm swings back by a large amount to gain energy.

5. The left leg bends to absorb the shock as the left arm swings around and the upper body twists.

6. As the left leg pushes off, the right leg takes a step to complete the turn and the upper body leans forward once again.

On a sloped surface, the character still needs to remain relatively vertical.

Going Up and Down Slopes

Another consideration when creating walks and runs is where the character is traveling. If the character is on a slope, the incline affects the posture of the character and how it walks or runs, because the character needs to remain relatively vertical against a sloping surface.

Walking Uphill

Because the character is essentially climbing against the force of gravity, a character walking uphill expends more energy than one walking on a flat surface. To do this, the character leans forward and swings the arms more to get a bit more momentum as it goes up the hill. The character also puts more effort as the leg lifts the body off of the ground, affecting the timing of the walk.

Walking Downhill

In a downhill situation, the character has gravity on his side. The force of gravity tends to pull the character forward. On an extreme slope, the character may simply slide down the hill. On a typical slope, the character leans back slightly and keeps the arms out to maintain balance. The knees also bend more as each foot sets down because the legs are acting as shock absorbers to dissipate the additional energy provided by gravity.

When walking uphill, the character leans forward and pumps the arms more to get a bit more momentum as it goes up the hill.

When walking downhill, the character leans back slightly and keeps the arms out to maintain balance.

Jumping

A jump is a good example of how the body can store and release maximum energy by bending and moving joints to their extremes. This particular jump happens with both feet and is somewhat symmetrical.

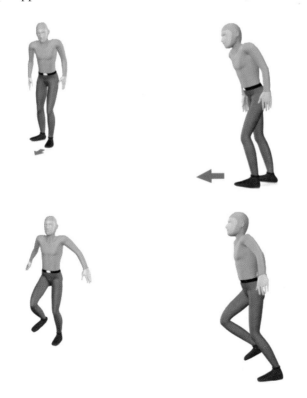

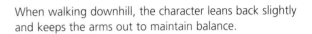

1. As is the case with many motions starting from a standing position, the jump usually begins with a small step—in this case, with the left foot. This sets the body in motion.

2. The left knee bends slightly as the right leg swings forward. The arms begin anticipating the jump by moving out and back slightly.

3. The left foot pushes off as
    both feet leave the ground
    for a little hop to anticipate
    the big jump. As this hap-
    pens, the arms continue their
    anticipation by moving
    upward to their full extreme,
    gaining maximum energy.

4. Both feet land and plant
    firmly on the ground as the
    knees bend quite a bit to
    absorb shock, but also gain
    maximum energy. The arms
    are already rotating forward
    at the shoulders, with the
    elbows extended to get the
    maximum pendulum effect.

5. The legs straighten out and
    push the body upward.
    Adding to this is the
    momentum of the arms,
    which continue rotating
    forward and pull the
    body upward.

6. As the body reaches the apex
    of the jump, the character
    pulls the legs up toward the
    chest. This is to gain maxi-
    mum momentum from the
    legs. The arms rotate forward
    as the torso leans forward.

7. The character lands with the feet ahead of the hips and the upper body still bent forward. The arms are back and out slightly to maintain balance.

8. The momentum of the body bends the knees to absorb the shock. The upper body bends as an additional shock absorber as the shoulders almost touch the knees. The arms swing forward like a pendulum.

9. The character stands.

Leaping

Although many people use the words *leap* and *jump* interchangeably, a leap has one foot forward at the beginning of the jump. It is like an extended step in a run and is usually the type of jump performed while running.

1. The character starts on a run. The leap starts with the left foot.

2. As the character plants the left foot, the arms swing back.

3. As the left knee bends, the left leg and arms swing forward and up, carrying the character's momentum upward.

4. The left leg pushes off as the character leaves the ground.

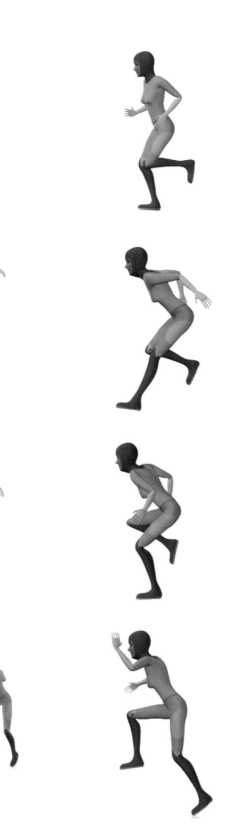

5. The right leg remains forward as the hips rotate forward and the arms move outward to maintain balance.

6. The character lands as the arms swing forward. At this point, the character can slow to a stop or keep running.

Dealing with External Forces

As you saw a bit earlier, characters need to deal with the outside world. This means they must interact with objects that usually create force on the body. Remember that forces have three major components: strength, direction, and point of application. From these three bits of information, you can pretty much determine how the body is going to react.

Lifting

If a character lifts an object with one hand, the weight of the object pulls the body out of balance, and the body leans to the side, away from the object. If a character is lifting with both hands, the body again leans away from the object to maintain balance. In this case, it leans back.

When a character is carrying a heavy object, it should be very difficult for the character to get moving. This means the character needs to take a series of small steps, gradually accelerating as the momentum of the

When lifting a heavy object with both hands, a character leans back to maintain balance.

weight carries the character forward. For the same reasons, the character also stops more slowly.

When a character is carrying something on one side of the body, the motion is a bit different, because only half of the body is under stress. While walking, the leg on the side of the weight remains fairly stiff as support, whereas the opposite leg moves more to compensate. This motion is similar to a limp, where one leg does more of the work and the other steps more slowly.

When a weight is on one side, half the body is under stress. The leg on the side of the weight remains stiff as the opposite leg takes a step.

Much like in a limp, the step using the leg on the weighted side of the body is short and the leg remains fairly stiff.

Pushing

In a push, the character gets behind the object, pressing the object with his hands and body and pressing against the ground to impart a force intended to move the object.

Friction is a big factor to consider when an object is being pushed. First, consider the behavior of friction. An object that is stationary has a lot more friction than one that is moving. Think of how much easier it is to continue pushing an object that is moving than it is to get it moving again if it stops.

Friction also applies to where the character's feet meet the ground. If the feet remain flat and stable against the ground, you have maximum friction between the character and the ground. If the feet start slipping, the character loses traction and the force of the push diminishes.

Of course this can be used for dramatic effect as well. To make an object appear extremely heavy, for example, you could have the character's feet slip constantly.

An object that is stationary has a lot more friction than one that is moving.

The force to pull the object still needs to be transmitted through the legs to the ground, so the character must place his feet firmly.

Pulling

The opposite of a push, the pull places the character ahead of the object being moved and connected to it by a handle or rope. The dynamics of a pull are a little bit different, because the character needs to hold the object with his hands. The force to pull the object still needs to be transmitted through the legs to the ground, so the character must place his feet firmly.

Getting Pulled

A character getting pulled or tugged by a rope experiences a very different motion and is a good example of an external force acting on the body. A rope pulls the character first at the arm, the force of which would throw the body out of balance. In fact, the whole motion is one of the character trying to maintain balance.

1. The character starts in a balanced pose, holding the rope in the right hand.

2. As the rope goes taut, it pulls the right arm and shoulder forward, twisting the upper body almost 180 degrees.

3. The force of the rope travels down the spine to the rest of the body so that the character leans forward. To maintain balance, the character pushes the body forward with the left foot, causing the right to take a step.

4. The shoulders move back about 45 degrees as the character pulls back against the rope to maintain balance. As he does this, the hips rotate around as he takes a second step with the left foot.

5. If the rope's pull remains constant, the character would continue to take more short hops. If the rope's tugs are more random, then the character would regain his balance, only to be pulled out of balance once the rope gets tugged again. The difference is that the character is expecting the second tug and leans back on both feet to counteract this.

Animating Rhythm and Dance

Dancing is something that intimidates a number of animators, but it actually can be quite fun. If the music is good, you get to listen to it all day, plus you get to dance in front of your computer and call it work. Of course, if the music is lousy, you still have to listen to it all day.

When animating dance moves, make sure everything happens to the beat. If your character's moves match the beat, then you can start the music anywhere and the dancing will work. The animated moves should all sync up regardless of where you place them in relation to the music.

Understanding Tempo

The key to animating dance is to let the tempo of the music drive the animation. Determining the tempo requires nothing more than a watch. Count the number of beats in six seconds of music. Multiply this by 10 to get the beats per minute (BPM). Once you have this, you can determine how many frames per beat of music. For example, a common BPM is 120.

At 24fps, the frames per beat would be 12:

24fps×60 sec = 1440 frames/min

1440fpm÷120bpm = 12 frames/beat

Here's a quick table for a range of tempos.

BPM	24fps	30fps
100	14.4 frames/beat	18 frames/beat
110	13	16.4
120	12	15
130	11	13.8
140	10.3	12.8

This table shows how, at some tempos, the frames per beat is a fractional number. This is one of the problems of a fixed frame rate. The best thing to do in this case is to round up or down to the nearest number and animate at that rate. Unless the shot is extremely long, the characters should sync up within a frame or two, which the audience will not notice.

Of course, if you want to be precise, or if the shot is particularly long, you can certainly read the track and mark down exactly which frames the beat hits. In this case, you are never more than a half frame off your sync.

It must be noted that characters can dance with or without music. If the character is dancing an unaccompanied jig of joy, then you can just pick a tempo and go with that. I usually pick 120BPM, simply because a half second per beat is easy.

The classic animation studios used to record their music to a fixed metronome. By knowing the beat of the music, the animators could animate even without the soundtrack. Warner Bros cartoons were usually animated at 120BPM, with most major moves occurring in multiples of 6 or 12 frames.

Figuring Out the Steps

Of course, all this math regarding BPM is secondary, because you first need to figure out how your character should move. Dance steps can be as simple as shaking the character's hips to the beat or as complex as tap-dancing.

Note

There's also the subject of the more formal modes of dancing, such as ballet, ballroom, modern, jazz, and tap. All these dances have a number of very unique steps and poses that require extensive reference to do properly. So instead, the following sections focus on more informal dance moves to explore all the basics of body movement, including balance, weight, and timing.

The one thing about dancing is that it lends itself to cyclical motion. That classic '70s dance craze, the Hustle, for example, is a series of steps that repeat, as is that mid-'90s craze, the Macarena. These two examples may be a bit dated and tacky, but they still point out that many dancers tend to repeat the same moves a number of times. You can animate a single shimmy or hip shake, for example, repeat it for a few measures, and then switch to other moves. Of course, dancers never repeat the same moves exactly the same way, so be sure to use the cycles as a basis for building unique motions on each cycle.

Dance moves can be very trendy. What is hip and cool in dance clubs and music videos this year will be totally passé the next. If you're animating for a music video, for example, you may need to duplicate a specific dance move. In this case, it is probably best to discuss the moves with a choreographer or videotape them as reference.

Getting the Hips Moving

Dancing is a very primal activity, and most of it starts with the hips. The simplest way to get a character dancing is to keep the feet planted and just get the hips moving. The easiest way is to create two poses: one with the hip neutral, the other with the hip out to the left. Animating between these two poses creates the foundation of the basic dance.

To give it a bit more life, you can mirror the extreme pose to create a pose with the hip out to the right. This gives you the opportunity to animate between the three as well as create patterns. You could go from right to left, or you could get more complex, such as right-right, left-left. The possibilities with these simple poses are endless.

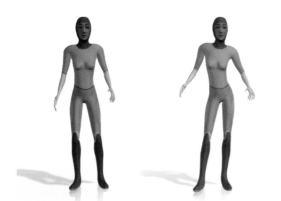

Here are two simple poses. Each has the character with the hips at one of two positions. Animating between these poses can create the foundation of a simple dance.

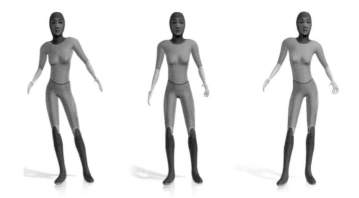

Adding a third pose opens up the possibilities. The character can go from right to left, right to right, and so on.

One thing about dancing is that it needs to be fluid and not mechanical. Simply inbetweening between two poses is not very fluid and gives you something that looks more like calisthenics than dancing. As was mentioned before, no dancer can hit the exact same pose twice. These poses are just a foundation; be sure to mix it up by varying the poses and overlapping the motions of the legs and hips.

Moving On Up

Now you can add to this foundation some upper-body motion. Perhaps the character moves her shoulders to the beat as well, or throws her hands above her head. All these moves can be layered on the basic hip motion. Again, by creating a few basic arm moves and a few basic hip moves, you give yourself a large palette from which to create a number of combinations. As with the hips, you need to mix up the poses to make sure that your upper-body motion isn't too repetitive.

When posing the upper body, be sure to keep the poses balanced. If the character has weight on the right leg, for example, the left leg is bent. This means the left hip is low as well, forcing the shoulders in the opposite direction to compensate.

Don't forget the head, which also bobs to the beat. Some dance moves, such as the Jerk, require extreme head motions. A good example of using the head would be the *Peanuts* TV specials of the late '60s. The characters had really big heads, and they danced by rocking their giant heads from side to side.

Adding a bit of arm motion adds to this foundation. The arms most often go in opposite directions (as the hips go right, the arms go left).

Stepping Out

Once you have some basic hip motion in action, it is very easy to see where dance steps can come in. One good way of looking at dancing is as a stylized walk: when the hips move, the character takes a step. A conga line is one example of this type of dancing. Many times, dance steps happen one to the beat, but the patterns vary widely. A common variation might be a sequence where the hips bounce twice for every step.

Another type of foot motion used widely in dance is the pivot. Rather than do a full step, a dancer may just pivot on the toes. This is the basis of the Twist, but it can be applied in many other contexts.

A simple dance move containing a single step. The character starts on both feet, executes a quick kick, and then returns to the original position.

A dance based on a walk. The character adds extra twist to the hips on each step and steps to the beat of the music.

This simple dance is accomplished by pivoting on the toes. First, the character pivots on both toes to the right, and then back to the left.

Adding Character

The way to make a dance move shine for any character is to add character, so you need to understand your character's personality and how it pertains to music. If your character is a stiff politician, it will dance much differently than a wild teenager. The character defines the dancing. As well, the choice of music will have an effect on the character. A cowboy might take kindly to country swing, for example, but resist techno music.

Martial Arts

Animating any type of high-action fighting, whether for games or feature films, can be one of the more difficult tasks an animator faces. Martial arts is an excellent example of the human body in motion.

There are dozens of martial arts moves. The following sections show you how to analyze and animate these types of motions. Additional reference for these types of moves might be found in a martial arts instructional video as well as your favorite Bruce Lee movie.

Posing for Martial Arts

A fighting character is usually posed in a coiled position, ready to strike or move out of the way at a moment's notice. A character involved in a fight is always trying to anticipate the unexpected.

For the body to be ready, the fighter usually keeps the knees bent, placing hips lower than normal. Bending the knees stores energy, much like a coiled snake. It also gives the fighter more options—straightening the leg allows the fighter to quickly jump; bending the leg allows him to quickly duck. If the legs were straight, for example, the fighter would need to bend the knees before jumping, wasting valuable time.

The fighter also uses his arms as defense. Boxers, for example, almost always keep both arms raised to deflect any blows to the face and upper body. Bending the arms also keeps them coiled and ready to throw a quick punch.

The Punch

A simple punch shows how even the simplest motion requires use of the entire body. Notice how the punch actually starts with the foot and moves upward through the body. This is just one example; punches can come in all different forms, depending on the character and the situation.

1. The basic punch starts from a fighting stance.

2. The character anticipates the punch by moving the arm back. The weight is on the back foot as well. A good boxer does not anticipate for too long, because this tells his opponent that the punch is coming. Alternatively, a drunken character might anticipate for a few seconds.

3. As the punch begins, the character takes a small step to place the weight on the forward foot. This allows the character to place weight on this foot for the actual punch.

4. The punch is thrown. The forward leg straightens to rotate the hips, which in turn, rotate the torso, shoulders, and arm. The arm extends to full length as it contacts the target.

5. After the punch, the arm rotates back as the character settles in to a stable stance.

The Kick

The kick is a good exercise for basic weight transfer and balance. It should be noted that a fighting kick is very different from a dance kick. A dance kick needs to just look good, whereas a fighting kick needs to place as much force as possible on the target.

1. The kick starts from a stable, balanced pose. The character's body turns 90 degrees during the move, so place the character accordingly.

2. The character kicks with the right foot, so he takes a step with the left foot to get some momentum.

3. As the right foot lifts off the ground, the shoulders twist to the left to maintain balance.

4. The torso leans back as the hips rotate upward. The right leg is bent at first, to give maximum power to the kick.

5. The right leg kicks forward. The hips are nearly vertical at this point, causing the torso to lean back toward horizontal. The right arm extends forward to counterbalance this weight. The left foot may also pivot as the body's momentum pulls it forward, rotating the body 90 degrees.

6. Weight shifts to the left leg as it touches the ground. The knee bends to absorb the weight of the body.

The Jump-Kick

A more active version of the kick is the jump-kick. This not only looks better in a film, but also allows a fighter to kick higher up on the opponent's body.

1. The jump-kick starts from a stable pose. This kick will be with the right leg.

2. To get things moving, the character takes a quick step with the right leg.

3. As the weight transfers to the right leg, the left leg swings around in a wide arc to give maximum momentum. The spine and shoulders twist to compensate.

4. As the left leg moves upward, it carries the entire body with it. The hips and shoulders rotate toward center and the right leg bends at the hip and knee to gain maximum energy for the kick.

5. The hips twist quickly as the right leg kicks out. In order to maintain balance, the spine and shoulders twist in the opposite direction and the arms move out from the body. The left leg simultaneously moves down in preparation for landing.

6. The character lands on the left leg, with the arms out to maintain balance. The left knee bends to absorb the shock of landing.

7. The right leg then touches the ground as the knee bends to take the weight of the body. The left leg takes a step, because the character's momentum still moves him forward.

Getting Hit

In martial arts and fight sequences, when one character throws a punch or a kick, it often is directed against another character. Knowing how to take a punch is as important as knowing how to throw one. When a sudden force, such as a punch, is directed at a character, the body first reacts at the point of contact, with the rest of the body following a few frames later, because it takes time for the force of the blow to travel through the body.

1. Before getting hit, the character is in a balanced pose.

2. When the blow lands against the side of the face, the force twists the head to the left, throwing the body off balance.

3. The head continues left as the force travels down the body. The character pivots on his toe.

4. The character takes a step and moves his arms out to maintain balance and recover.

Conclusion

As you can see, the body is a complex system, and animating realistic motion is a complex task. As with any complex task, breaking down a character's motions into components will make the job manageable. Focus on the subsystems of the body (arms, legs, and so on) to understand how they interact with the body as a whole.

CHAPTER 6

Acting

Animators are, in many respects, actors who use a mouse, pencil, or clay to bring a character to life. An actor is a natural show-off, someone who always wants to be in the spotlight. Animators tend to hide behind their CRTs and light tables, but the performances they create must have the same vitality as any created in live action.

The animator makes characters communicate, not only with each other, but also with the audience. Characters must not only tell a story, but they must tell it in a believable and entertaining manner. When the audience pays for a ticket to your film, switches on your TV show, or downloads your movie off the Internet, they are expecting to be entertained, enlightened, and amused.

Bringing your character to life in a convincing manner means understanding the techniques of acting—being able to think and breathe like your character. When you truly step into a character, the actual act of animating becomes a bit of a blur. You become the conduit from the character to the mouse.

Acting Versus Animating

Plenty of people and schools can teach you how to act. These can be of great value to an animator. As you become more involved with creating characters, you can draw upon many techniques from the art of acting.

Acting, however, is fundamentally different from animation. Acting happens in real time, usually in front of an audience. Actors need to learn how to deal with the here and now. If a fellow actor flubs the line, a good actor is quick enough to cover the faux pas flawlessly. Because actors must operate in real time, they cannot go back and fix just a couple of frames; they have to re-create the entire performance.

Animation is much more of a solitary pursuit—most of the time it's just you and the computer. Animating is like acting in slow motion. Rather than act in real time, you do it a frame at a time. You go through many of the processes that an actor goes through, but the actual motions are translated through the mouse into the computer. Animators have the luxury of going back over a performance frame by frame until they consider it perfect.

Acting and Story

The characters that you animate are the storytellers. They need to convey the script to the audience in a convincing and entertaining manner. The greatest story in the world can be ruined if it is told by a poor storyteller. To make the story jump off the screen, you need to understand the story, story structure, and how each scene moves the story forward.

Each scene has an objective—a point it needs to get across. Each character within the scene also has an objective. A policeman, for example, wants to take the convict to jail. The convict's objective is freedom. How these two objectives work out determines how the story progresses. If the criminal escapes, you have *The Fugitive*. If he goes to jail, you have *The Shawshank Redemption*. When you animate a scene, be clear as to your character's objectives and how they affect the story.

Know Your Tools

Acting is pure right-brain activity. You need to remain totally "in the moment" so that you can truly become one with your character. In a Zen sense, when you connect with the right side of the brain, your character flows through you and subconsciously takes control of the mouse. You don't have to think consciously about how a character is moving; it just moves. Constantly stepping out of this mindframe to solve technical problems or to consult the manual breaks the flow and cheapens your animation.

Before you ever start acting for animation, you need to learn mastery over your chosen software tools. You should be able to set and modify keyframes automatically, without conscious thought. Your characters also need to be rigged properly so that they are rock solid and easy to manipulate. You don't want technical issues to crop up during animation and break your creative flow.

In addition, a good knowledge of human motion, which is discussed later in this book, also helps you remain in the moment. You should be able to construct natural, balanced poses without much effort. Thinking about the pose is a left-brain activity. Don't go there.

Know Your Audience

One thing that tends to be overlooked is the audience. If you are animating a Saturday morning children's show, your acting choices are probably different than they are if you're animating for a late-night comedy show. Knowing your audience helps you create a performance that will be understood and accepted.

Don't, however, fall into the trap of letting the audience dictate the performance. Pandering is not allowed. Don't make obvious choices. If you do what the audience expects all the time, they become bored. Always think of the unexpected turn—what are you going to do in this performance to make it interesting and keep the audience entertained? Your audience must understand and empathize with the character. You must fully understand your character and be true to its personality. If the audience empathizes with your character's plight, then you have them won.

Know Your Characters

The foundation of good acting is understanding who your character is and what makes it tick. If you truly know your character, you innately know how and when the character is going to move and how it reacts to the world. Understanding a character can be a long and involved process, and actors use many techniques to accomplish this. The first thing you need to do is answer a few simple questions about the character.

Some of the questions that are already dictated by the character's design include the following:

How tall?

Fat or skinny?

Healthy or sickly?

What ethnicity?

How old?

Sloppy or neat?

Etc.

Other questions are more personal and internal:

How smart?

Are there goals and dreams?

Any addictions?

Morning person or night person?

Family background?

Favorite foods?

Etc.

These questions are really just the tip of the iceberg. To truly understand your character, you will need to write a character description and a biography.

Character Descriptions

A character description puts down on paper who the character is. Many times the writer does this as part of the writing process. If you are animating a one-shot character in a commercial, however, you may have to come up with your own description.

A character description is a paragraph or less and goes over the basics of the character. Usually, it covers just the important things, such as age, sex, and personality. Here are two character descriptions for *Karen & Kirby*, a series of interstitials I produced for Warner Bros.

Karen Jones—Karen is 9 years old and the second most popular girl in school. She's high maintenance and used to having things her way, the easy way. This is not to say she's spoiled. Karen is very likable, and absolutely everyone likes Karen. Because of this, things just naturally tend to go her way. She looks to Kirby as a brother and trusted companion. Karen lives with her dad in a low-slung suburban bungalow that's quite stylish and very neat.

Kirby Derwood—Kirby is 10 years old and the second most *un*popular kid in school. Clever and intelligent, he takes great delight in creating very complex solutions to very simple problems, which causes things to blow up in his face. Kirby is a bit of a neurotic—if things don't go as planned, he tends to freak out. This happens a lot. Kirby lives with his dad in a small Airstream trailer parked in Karen's backyard that's very cramped and somewhat messy.

Exercise #1: Adding Personality

Take a character that you've modeled and give it a personality by writing a brief character description. This should be about a paragraph long.

Character Biographies

Many times, you can get by with just a simple description. This is fine for short-form projects, such as commercials and interstitials. If you are animating a longer-form project, such as a feature, you may want to create a more in-depth biography that really nails down the character's personality.

A biography is more formal than a description, and is longer—usually a page or two long. Like the description, it gives the basics of the character but with a lot more depth. It might go into a character's education, family, traumatic events, or anything else that has shaped the character's life.

Some people go totally overboard in a character biography, writing what amounts to a good-sized FBI file. For a feature film, this is probably a good idea, because the character needs to be as fleshed out as possible before animation begins. If your character is going to show up for 15 seconds in a malted milk ball commercial, though, you'll do just fine without knowing the names of the character's maternal grandparents.

For characters in a TV series, the biography is constantly evolving. Sometimes it's best not to lock things down because the writers and animators invariably discover new things about the characters as the series progresses. When *Rocko's Modern Life* was pitched, there was no information in the character descriptions about Heffer's parents. In the first season, Vince Calandra wrote a terrific story about how Heffer's parents were actually wolves who adopted him with the plan of fattening him up for dinner. Instead of eating him, however, they fell in love with him. This episode was both hilarious and poignant, and it added a whole new dimension and direction to Heffer's character.

Exercise #2: Creating a Character Biography

Take the character description you just created and flesh it out into a full-fledged biography. The biography should be at least a page long and give an in-depth view of your character's personality. Who is this character? Where was he born? Where did he grow up? What are his parents like? Does he have siblings? What are they like? What sort of childhood did he have? Who's his best friend? Who's his greatest enemy? What is the character's biggest fear? Greatest desire? You can ask zillions more questions; ask as many as you need to truly nail down the personality of your character.

Acting Technique

Once you finally understand your character, you need to put that knowledge into action by acting and performing the character. Acting is an art form, and like any art form, it has a number of core principles. These principles, however, are only the tip of the iceberg. As with any art form, the deeper you explore, the more you see there is to learn.

Creating Empathy

The big goal of an animator, as well as of the writers, is to create empathy for the character. *Empathy* means the audience emotionally connects with the character on some level and identifies with him. This is not to be confused with *sympathy*, where the audience simply feels sorry for someone. When a character evokes sympathy, members of the audience say "I pity that guy." When the audience feels empathy, members of the audience can say "I know how that guy feels—I've been there myself." An empathic character plays to the heart.

Say that you need to animate the oldest gag in the book: a character slipping on a banana peel. You can have the character's feet fly out from under him, have him land on his kiester, and then get up and move along. Pretty boring, and the audience will not feel much empathy for the character.

Instead, try to bring out your character by showing a side of his personality to the audience. This enables the audience to go beyond the simple action to feel what your character is feeling. If the character is an extremely proud person, he might get up quickly and look around to make sure he didn't embarrass himself in front of others. If the character is starving to death, then perhaps he'll pull the banana peel off the bottom of his shoe and eat it, turning an unfortunate incident into a humorous blessing.

Villains also need to generate empathy. How many times have you seen a cartoon where the villain was completely evil with no redeeming qualities? These villains are usually two dimensional and not very interesting. Just like the hero, villains also need to get the audience on their side. The scariest villains are the ones who appear real to the audience. A villain is essentially a hero with one fatal flaw. The character might be an everyday individual who turns bad because of something that happened in his past to make him evil. This dark past would be the fatal flaw. A great example is Darth Vader, from the *Star Wars* movies. He was a hero until he joined the Dark Side—his fatal flaw was his desire for power.

Think of Kathy Bates in *Misery*. She created a very real and very scary character. Most people know people who are big fans of something—an actor, a TV series, a movie, or, in this case, characters in a series of books written by an author (played by James Caan). When Kathy Bates's character learns that the book series (along with its main character) will essentially be killed, she does what she must to protect them. Her fatal flaw is an overwhelming love for a fictional character. She detains James Caan and forces him to keep her beloved character alive by writing more books. It's almost like it's her motherly duty to protect those characters. Despite her fatal flaw, the audience identifies with her, both as an ardent fan and a protective mother.

When you animate, try to get the audience to understand your character and what it is feeling. Go beyond the actions to dig deep into the character's personality and find actions that define your character.

Creating Inspiration

Animation is performing, and a good performance is an inspired performance. One starting point for creating inspiration is a concept Stanislavski, the originator of the modern style of realistic acting, described as the "magic if." The "magic if" asks the question "What would I do if I were in these circumstances?"

The answer to this simple question can be a springboard to creativity and inspiration. As an animator you get the chance to be someone else for the day—a fictional character, a cartoon. In a true cartoon world, what WOULD you do if you had an anvil dropped on your head? For the cartoon character, this sort of stuff happens all the time and is perfectly normal. When you put yourself totally in the character's environment and circumstances, it inspires you.

In a true cartoon world, what WOULD you do if you had an anvil dropped on your head? When you put yourself totally in the character's environment, it inspires you.

In many respects, this technique is a lot like play-acting. A child truly believes her doll is real. It is the job of animators to make the digital props and sets real to themselves. By using the "magic if," animators grant themselves permission to "believe" in these imaginary objects.

Creating Movement

Until a character moves, it is nothing but a nicely modeled mannequin. Animating a character—bringing it to life—requires that you move it. The first thing a novice animator does is start moving body parts around to see what happens. This trial and error approach can have its moments, but a professional animator needs a much larger arsenal. First, you need to understand that characters always move for a reason. Those reasons are almost always emotionally driven. You cannot "will" emotions. In life, emotions result from stimuli, which affect the character's senses and evoke an emotional response.

The emotions the character feels dictate the type and quality of the motion: a sad character moves much differently than a happy one, for example. Being able to convey a character's emotions through motion is what makes an animator great.

Different emotions cause a character to move differently.

Most of the time, people do not think about the individual actions they perform. When you walk, you usually do not think about placing one foot in front of another. If you're in love, you're thinking about your lover—while you happen to be walking. The emotions dictate the character of the walking motions.

When a comedian tells a joke, you laugh; you do not think, "Now I'm going to laugh." This is the key to good animation. Your character's movements need to be unforced and natural. When you are truly animating, you are not really thinking about the individual motions. Instead, you are in a creative flow, where the motion just happens as a consequence of the emotions your character is feeling.

Cause and Effect

Cause and effect drive a story. A story is a sequence of events. Each event has an effect on the next. Cause and effect also drive how a character is animated.

The cause can be any sort of action, from a force of nature to the actions of another character. The effect is how your character deals with those actions. Your character smells smoke—he looks around for flames. Your character sees a bully walking down the street—he decides to turn in the other direction. Your character hears funky music—he starts dancing.

Think of how cause and effect work with animation. If you simply create a pose with a bent arm, the audience reads the pose as a character with a bent arm. If instead you create a form like a bent arm with a specific force in mind, the bent arm now becomes a form with intent. The force causes the arm to bend, and the resulting pose is the effect of that force.

Other times, the cause of an action is internal—drawn from a memory. A character remembers a pleasant childhood moment and smiles. A starving character remembers the taste of apple pie and his mouth waters. In these cases, the eyes still matter. A character remembering something always moves its eyes as it searches for the memory.

Object of Attention

As we move through the day, our attention shifts from place to place, from object to object. Things happen. Those things demand attention.

Right now, your attention is focused on this book. You're exercising only those parts of the body that are used for reading. The rest of your body is relaxed. If the telephone were to suddenly ring, your attention would shift away from this book to the telephone. You would then exercise those parts of the body needed to travel to the phone and pick up the receiver. You would forget about the book momentarily as you focused completely on the phone.

Lee Strasberg, the father of method acting, would say that, in this case, the individual's object of attention has changed from the book to the phone. The object of attention is a basic building block with which both actors and animators work. By having the character concentrate on an object, which represents the task at hand, the animator establishes a sense of belief that the character is truly involved in what he is doing.

When a cat toys with a catnip toy in the kitchen, it uses only those muscles necessary to concentrate on the object of attention: the toy. The cat is simply trying to accomplish a specific "task": to conquer the toy. All other muscles are completely relaxed.

When the character is reading the book, he's exercising only those parts of the body that are used for reading.

When the phone rings, the character's attention completely shifts to the phone. He momentarily forgets about the book.

If the dog dashes into the kitchen looking for a drink, the cat's body suddenly changes its demeanor as she focuses on the new object of attention: the dog. The cat may tense up and arch her back, but she still uses only those muscles necessary to concentrate on her new object of attention. The cat's task has changed and she has momentarily forgotten the toy; her new task is to put the dog in its place.

The dog's object of attention, which had been "water," now becomes "the cat," and his original objective to "drink water" now becomes "growl at the cat." The dog is using only those muscles necessary to accomplish this task. He is focused on the cat, not the water.

Exercise #3: Changing the Object of Attention

Create a short scene where a character is focused on doing one task, and then switches his object of attention to another. Be sure the character is completely focused on each task. Once you animate this, extend the scene by shifting the focus back to the first task.

Clarity

Making your character 100% focused on the task at hand gives your performance clarity. The audience knows exactly what the character is thinking at any given moment. Even when a character is distracted momentarily, it focuses 100% of its attention on the distraction for that fleeting moment.

Take the dog and cat situation a step further. Perhaps the dog becomes indecisive—he really needs that drink but still has to deal with that pesky cat. If you were to split the difference, the dog would focus 50% of the way between the cat and the water. The audience then wonders, "Why is the dog staring into space?"

Even in his indecision, the dog needs to switch between objects of attention—100% on the water, 100% on the cat. He looks longingly at the water, and then turns back to growl at the cat. When he is looking at the water, he can really imagine that cool drink. When he is facing the cat, he is totally absorbed in that task.

The dog really needs that cool drink …

…but he also needs to deal with the cat. Even when your character cannot make up his mind, he is fully focused on one possibility or the other.

If your character is 100% focused in the scene, the performance is crystal clear. If the character is not focused, the performance is muddy. Even when your character cannot make up its mind, it is fully focused on one possibility or the other. Of course, the audience needs to be in on the indecision as well. Be sure to hold your poses long enough so the audience can read them. Once the poses are clear to the audience, you can switch back and forth between them more quickly.

Exercise #4: Focusing on a Single Object

Create a scene where a character needs to decide between two objects (soup and a sandwich, for example). As the character decides, shift the object of attention from one to the other and make sure the character is completely focused on only one object at a time.

Simplicity

Another way to achieve clarity is through simplicity. An old animation adage is "one thing at a time." This is similar to the concept of attention, but it also helps clarify the individual actions. A character trips, then falls, and then gets up—it doesn't do them all at once.

You also should be clear as to what the individual action represents. Don't animate anger—that's too broad and general. What exactly is the character angry at? It's better to animate "I hate my boss." This simplifies the emotion as well as it gives your character focus. To give the anger even more depth, add the survival objective "I am angry at my boss, but I need my job to survive." This adds even more depth to the emotion so the audience can truly empathize with your character.

In addition, try to simplify each of your character's poses and actions to keep them as clear as possible. The actions are like the links of a chain. They all fit together sequentially. If each action is clear and easily read, then that link of the chain is strong. An overly complex pose or action could possibly break the chain and lose the audience.

The Moment Before

One aspect of a character that is often overlooked is what the character was doing just before the scene started. Imagine a character entering a locker room. Is the character coming in off the street? Coming back from a heavy workout? Returning from a losing game? Each one of these situations affect how the character carries itself when it enters the scene. Knowing what happened in the moments before this moment helps you keep your character focused.

Exercise #5: Animating a Prior Event

This one is simple. Animate a character walking into a room. By the character's motions, make it clear to the audience what happened immediately before the character entered.

In each of these images, what happened just before the character entered the scene?

Status

When animating multiple characters in a scene, you need to determine their status in relation to each other. Understanding who is "top dog," so to speak, helps tremendously in guiding the interactions between your characters.

A servant always defers to the master. In politics, everyone is expected to stand when the President walks into the room. A drill sergeant dominates his recruits. These are all extreme examples, but status is important in any society, and it translates to every aspect of our dealings with others, no matter how subtle. One character is always more dominant, and others are more submissive.

There is also a status transaction, which happens regardless of rank and file and has to do with who is commanding the scene at the time. If you handle your poses in such a way that clearly illustrates who is in control of the scene, the emotions will be more easily read. An example would be a man proposing to a woman. He is in control of the scene when proposing, and then she is in control with her response. No one is necessarily higher than the other in a sense of society or rank and file, but each has a command of the scene at different times.

Status is displayed through body posture. The character with the higher status usually stands tall and projects his energy outward with a steady gaze. A submissive character leans forward and gazes down, sends his energy toward the floor.

A good example of status would be in the film *Ghandi*. Normally, a prisoner is accorded a lower status than the guards, but when Ghandi is sent to prison, he maintains his high status through the position of his body. His actions are always centered and very self-assured as compared to his captors'.

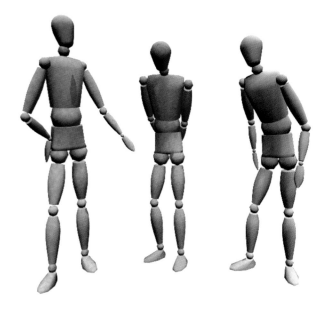

Which character has the higher status?

Givens

Whenever you work with a character, things are "given" to you to work with. These are the things you cannot change about the character. You may or may not agree with some of the decisions made before you took control of the character, but you need to accept these givens and use them to your advantage.

Voices are one of the biggest givens for the animator. Typically, this is positive, because a good voice performance is an excellent foundation from which to build convincing animation. Big conflicts can arise, however, when an animator doesn't agree with the voicing of the character.

Other givens include the design of the character, the virtual sets, and other constraints. If you are integrating a character with live action, you may have to go as far as to match your character's movements with that of a live-action actor.

With any of these givens, the trick is to use them to your advantage. Working with the director may help to clarify the choices that were made before the work got to you. Many times the cleverest solutions come out of limitations.

Acting and the Body

Knowing the specifics of how the body moves as it reacts to stimuli is something every animator should know. The body can be broken up into a few major parts. The head and face are important, as well as the hands. The spine and its position also factor in to how a character is perceived.

The Head

The head is the center of intellect. The position of the head determines, to a great deal, how the audience perceives a character. Cocking the head to the side throws the body off center. Generally, this can indicate confusion but also curiosity. If a character is affirming something, his head may nod slightly as if to say "yes." Conversely, the head may shake from side to side slightly when a character is in disagreement.

Head cocked to one side can indicate curiosity.

The head raised high is more childlike.

Lowering the head indicates authority—on a kid, it's downright creepy.

When the head is held up, exposing the throat, it indicates a more naive and childlike character. Kids are short—they look up a lot. When the head is down, hiding the neck, the character is more authoritative and serious. Think of Jerry Lewis. When he was young and paired with Dean Martin in the '50s, his character was that of an innocent and naive man. He kept his head high. When Jerry Lewis hosted the telethon, he had to be a lot more compelling. In this instance, he lowered his head.

The Shoulders

Shoulders often express mood or emotion. In some respects, their motions are related to those of the hands, but shoulders can express themselves outside of hand motions. The shrug is a good example of expression through shoulder motions. A character pushing its way through a crowd may lead with the shoulders, much as a linebacker does.

The general position of the shoulders can also indicate mood. Slumped shoulders indicate weariness, while squared shoulders indicate alertness. If a character is defending itself, it turns the body and raises the shoulder facing the attacker. This presents a smaller target to the attacker than if the character were to face it directly.

Slumped shoulders can indicate weakness or weariness.

Squared shoulders are more forceful.

Shoulders can also indicate emotion, such as in this shrug.

The Hands

The hands are one of the most expressive parts of the body. In most instances, they communicate more than the face. The hands can gesticulate over an area of several feet, whereas the face covers only a few inches. Of course, in film, the close-up can place more emphasis on the face, but most shots usually involve the body.

The big question with most animators is what to do with the hands. Some hand positions are universal in their meaning. Hands folded across the chest, for example, indicate that a character is closing itself off. Hands clasped behind the back are an indication of respect and lower status. A character with one hand on the hip might appear relaxed, whereas both hands on the hips make a character appear to be confrontational.

Hands above the head are more intellectual. Where the hands are raised in relation to the body can also communicate a great deal about the character's demeanor. If the character raises his hands above the shoulders, it is a more intellectual gesture. Anxiety is a very intellectual emotion, and anxious people tend to hold their hands fairly high. Hands held lower are more primitive. A construction worker gesturing at a pretty girl will position the hands below the chest.

Hands held lower are more primitive.

Hands near the chest are more emotive.

Hands above the head are more intellectual.

The Spine and Posture

The spine is very important to the overall look of the body. The spinal cord is where all the sensory data from the body is transmitted to the brain. The spinal cord also has a bit of its own intelligence—many reflex actions actually happen in the spinal cord rather than the brain.

Posture is a very important indicator of a character and its demeanor. Your mom always told you to stand up straight for a reason. A proud character stands tall and arches its back to stick the chest out. Conversely, a depressed character tends to hunch over more. As the body ages, the spine stiffens, which makes it difficult for older characters to twist the spine and turn around.

A character's posture is a strong indicator of its mood.

The spine also figures prominently into status negotiations between characters. A character with high status stands taller and straighter. This goes pretty much for any character with higher self-worth. Such a character tends to keep its weight at the center of its body, near the hips. Characters with lower status subconsciously lower themselves by bending their spines and lowering their shoulders.

The Spine and *Chakras*

When you're trying to understand a character, you need to understand where on the body the character's personality emanates. One way to look at this is with a bit of Eastern philosophy and the concept of a *chakra*.

The word *chakra* is Sanskrit for wheel or disk and signifies one of seven basic energy centers in the body. Each of these centers correlates to major nerve ganglia branching forth from the spinal column. The *chakras* also correlate to levels of consciousness, developmental stages of life, colors, sounds, body functions, and much, much more.

For animators, the best way to understand this is that the more primitive the emotion, the lower it sits on the spine. This little tidbit can be used as a guide to animating a character. The character's personality emanates most strongly from that point on the body. Primitive personalities, such as Rocky Balboa's, emanate from low on the body. People who love others tend to emanate their personalities from the heart, or the middle *chakra*. An intellectual's personality, such as Woody Allen's, emanates from the head.

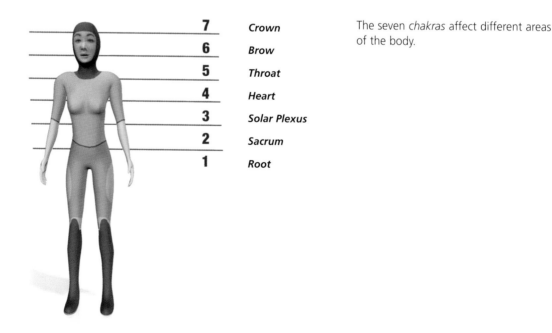

7	Crown
6	Brow
5	Throat
4	Heart
3	Solar Plexus
2	Sacrum
1	Root

The seven *chakras* affect different areas of the body.

In general, the three lower *chakras* are connected to the main needs—of survival, fertility, and the free will—whereas the four higher *chakras* are in connection with a character's psychological makeup and define love, communication, and knowledge, as well as spirituality.

The Seven *Chakras* and Personality

CHAKRA	ISSUES	GOALS	DESIRES	PERSONALITY
1 – Root	Survival, grounding	Self-preservation	Stability, health, prosperity	Physical
2 – Sacrum	Sexuality, emotions, desire	Self-gratification	Pleasure, sexuality, feeling	Emotional
3 – Solar Plexus	Power, will	Self-definition	Spontaneity, purpose, self-esteem	Egoist
4 – Heart	Love, relationships	Self-acceptance	Compassion, acceptance, relationships	Social
5 – Throat	Communication	Self-expression	Communication, creativity, resonance	Creative
6 – Brow	Intuition, imagination	Self-reflection	Perception, interpretation, imagination	Perceptive
7 – Crown	Awareness	Self-knowledge	Wisdom, knowledge, consciousness	Intellectual

Exercise #6: Animating Dialogue Through Chakras

Take a simple line of dialogue, such as "Boy, I'm really tired," or "These pretzels are making me thirsty," and animate the line three different ways. First, animate the character from the lower *chakras*. Next, animate the character from the middle ones, and finally from the upper ones. You'll soon discover that each zone of the body communicates the line differently.

Other Techniques

There are dozens of other acting techniques and theories about acting. Basically, they all boil down to psychology and how to get the body to do things it would not normally do. How many people can actually cry on cue? Not many, I imagine. An actor with sufficient training, however, can do such a task reliably. As an animator, you never need to cry on cue, but understanding some of these techniques can help you empathize with your character and animate it better.

Sense Memory

If you have ever been really hungry, the thought of food was probably enough to actually make your mouth water. This is an example of your senses remembering the taste of the food and your body responding accordingly by activating your salivary glands. As an animator, you can use your sense memory to conjure up emotions and actions for your character.

If your character is hungry, try to remember the last time you were truly hungry. How did it feel? Did it make you light-headed? How did you move? Slowly? Were you easily agitated? When an animator does a sensory exercise such as this, he may find emotional responses occurring that he may not have anticipated.

Animal Exercises

If you are having problems trying to understand a character, you may need to look at it from a different angle. One method is to try re-creating the character as an animal. What animal does your character move and act like?

When doing this exercise, you need to be very specific in your observation. Go to the zoo and watch the animal for at least an hour. What is the animal's posture? How does he move? When does he move? Why does he move? Can you imagine what the animal might be thinking?

If you can, try to physically imitate the animal's motions. Again, as specific as possible. Look into the animal's eyes. Does it seem intelligent? Tame? Wild? Dangerous? Try to transfer the animal's thoughts to your own thoughts.

Of course, in animation, you often have to animate animals themselves. Many times, this demands the same sort of observations. In some cases, however, the animals don't act like the bodies they inhabit. Think of the elephant "Shep" in the live-action remake of *George of the Jungle*. The elephant was raised as a pet and acted more like a dog than an elephant—even going as far as to fetch a "stick," which was actually a six-foot-long log. In this case, a couple of hours spent watching your dog would be very helpful.

Affective Memory

Using "affective memory" is one of the most widely known procedures in all of "method" acting. Simply put, it tries to put an actor as close to a character as possible by asking him to recall a similar event or experience in his own life.

This technique is used most notably in the sorts of scenes that expect an actor to dig really deep—those scenes with a very strong emotional content, such as when a character loses his best friend to murder, a character's spouse demands a divorce, or a character discovers he has an incurable disease. In these situations it may be necessary for the animator to find similar experiences in his own life, and be first willing, and then able to relive those experiences as the character is animated.

This technique is most often mentioned when characters are in stressful and traumatic situations. But affective memory can be used for lighter moments as well. If your character wins the lottery, try to recall a moment in your life when you had a similar experience that both shocked you and made you joyously happy—perhaps the moment you got accepted into animation school!

Conclusion

As you have seen, acting is very important to the animator's craft. Study your characters and understand them fully before you tackle a scene. When animating, be conscious of your character's personality and the objectives of the scene. The audience needs to be able to relate to the characters on the screen—characters always needs to evoke empathy from the audience. Without empathy, you're sunk.

CHAPTER 7

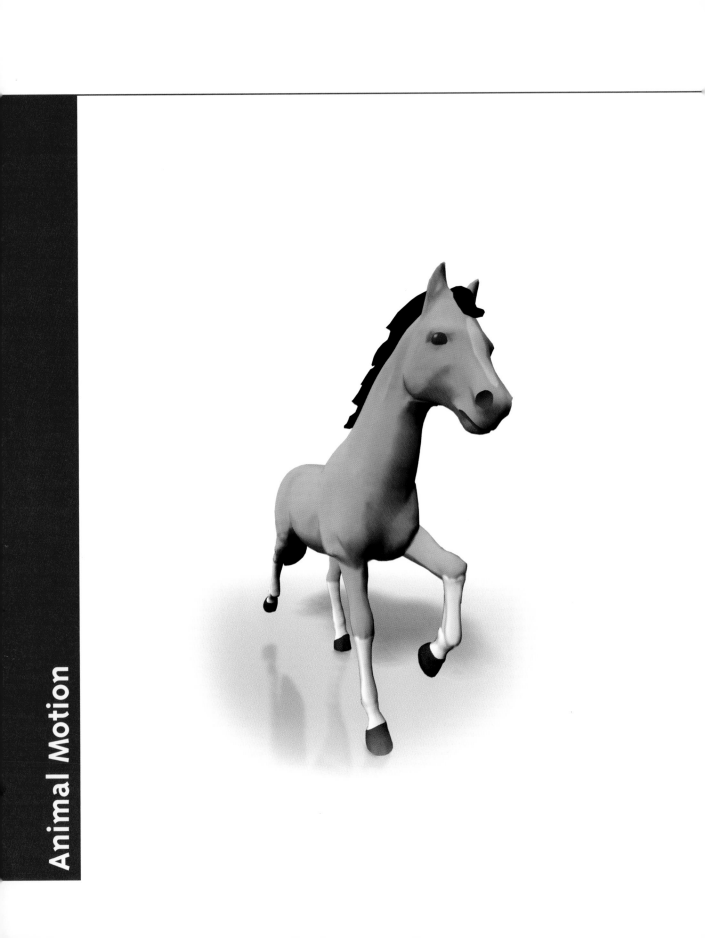

Animal Motion

A nimals are quite common in animation. Many times animators need to bring four-legged creatures to life. The anatomy of most four-legged animals, as well as birds, reptiles, and dinosaurs, is quite different from our primate podiatry. This chapter gives you the essentials you need to know to animate most of the major types of animals.

In addition to the basics, each animal has different ways of moving, depending on the size, shape, and purpose of an animal. Small animals tend to move faster than large ones; predators move differently than prey. When animating animals, it is always a good idea to go to the source, so to speak, and get lots of reference for your animation. A trip to the zoo or a good nature documentary can help you understand how each animal moves.

Four-Legged Mammals

The skeleton of a four-legged mammal is similar to the skeleton of a human in that they both have four limbs, and those limbs contain the same bones. The lengths and arrangements of the bones, however, are where the differences lie.

Take a dog, for example. Whereas humans walk on their heels and toes, the dog walks on only his toes. The dog's "heel" is far above the ground—approximately where a human knee would be. The dog's knee is actually even higher up, as are the thighs and hips. The front legs are similar to our arms, but again, the dog walks on his fingers. Like the heel, the dog's "wrist" is far above the ground, with the elbow even higher.

Heavy-set animals, like the hippo, appear to have short, stubby legs, because the animal's skin tends to hang lower, obscuring the upper part of the leg. A skeleton for a hippo looks much like the skeleton for any other four-legged creature, except the upper parts of the legs are hidden inside the body.

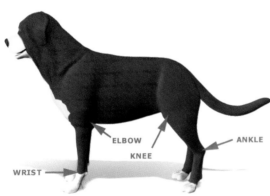

A dog walks on bones that are human toes and fingers, with the wrist and ankle above the ground.

On a hippo, the elbows and knees are located near the belly, with the upper parts of the leg hidden under the heavy skin.

The center of gravity is usually located halfway between the hips and shoulders.

The center of gravity is also slightly different for a four-legged beast. Rather than being located at the hips, it is farther up on the body, roughly centered between the front and back legs. The center of gravity is important in animation. If the animal were to leap, for example, the entire body's rotation would center around this point. An animal such as a dachshund has a center of gravity near the middle of the spine. Other animals, such as cheetahs or greyhounds, have large chests, placing the center of gravity further forward on the body. The head also plays a role in determination of center of gravity. A giraffe's long neck places its center of gravity farther up the spinal column, at the back of the shoulders.

Skeletons for Quadrupeds

A quadruped is simply any animal that has four legs. A skeleton for a
quadruped is fairly easy to build. A quadruped skeleton is similar to a
human skeleton. The animal still has hips and shoulders connected via a
spinal column, but the spine is aligned horizontally rather than vertically.
Another factor to consider is that that the bones for the limbs are of differing lengths than those in humans.

A quadruped skeleton is similar to a human skeleton, but
aligned horizontally rather than vertically.

IK chains are the best way to build the legs, with the feet
attached hierarchically.

The center of gravity may cause you to set up the hierarchy of a
quadrupedal skeleton slightly differently. Because both the front and back
legs move equally, the hierarchy can be set up with the center of the
spine as the parent. Having the root of the hierarchy here makes it easier
to do things such as bending the spine. For many four-legged animals,
having the root of hierarchy at the hips also works well.

Most four-legged mammals also have tails. A tail is easy to configure as a
simple chain of linked bones connected to the hips. These are typically
animated using Forward Kinematics.

To keep animation simple, some animators like to tie the many bones of
a tail to a single set of sliders that control the bones' rotations. This is as
easy as linking the rotation of each bone to a slider. Moving one slider
rotates many bones.

An animal's tail can be deformed by
using a simple chain of bones.

Analysis of a Four-Legged Walk

A four-legged walk is very similar to the two-legged variety, but multiplied by two. The creature's legs still rock back and forth at the hips, but the upper body motion happens parallel to the ground rather than perpendicular to it. Whereas human shoulders rock back and forth on the vertical axis, a dog's "shoulders" rock back and forth horizontal to the ground as the front paws move back and forth.

A four-legged walk is also similar to a two-legged walk in that the hips and shoulders have rotations that mirror each other. When the right hip is forward, the left shoulder is back, and vice versa. This action usually varies a bit in that the front and back legs might be offset by a few frames. Notice how the spine curves much like a human spine and that the left shoulder and leg are back, mirroring the hip pose. This means that the left front leg, too, is about to plant.

As the legs move forward through the step, the legs that are not currently planted on the ground (the free legs) move forward. The rear legs are fairly similar to a human's, bending at the knee in much the same fashion. The front legs, however, are actually jointed so that they bend forward, much like a bird's. This dictates a slightly different lift motion for the front legs. At this point, the spine is straight when viewed from the top, but it may bow or arch a bit more when viewed from the side. This is character dependent. A dilapidated horse's back may sag quite a bit.

This step has the right rear leg forward and about to plant the foot.

Halfway through the step, the free legs are moving forward. Notice how the front leg's joint causes a different bend in the leg.

The legs then move through the step and plant the free feet, repeating the first step. In addition to this, a four-legged animal can have several different gaits: the walk, the trot, the canter, and the gallop. The animal varies the timing and rhythm of its steps as it moves faster and faster. In the walk, the animal's legs behave very much like the arms and legs of a human—if the right rear leg is back, the right front leg is forward, with the opposite happening on the left. This changes as the strides change, however. By the time the creature has reached full gallop, the front legs are in sync—going forward and back nearly in unison, with the back legs operating as a mirror to the front.

Animating a Four-Legged Walk Cycle

A quadrupedal skeleton can be made to walk quite easily. It is a simple matter of getting the back legs to walk much like a two-legged character's and then adding in the front leg motions. When animating a four-legged walk, you need to ensure that both pairs of legs move the same distance with each step. If the back legs have a larger stride than the front, for example, the back of the creature will soon be ahead of the front.

The timing of the walk is also important. As with humans, timing is dependent on a number of factors, including the size of the animal, the type of gait, and its mood. Larger animals take more frames for each step—an elephant steps much more slowly than a mouse, for example. The animal's mood is also a big factor; a tired dog walks much more slowly than a happy one.

Exercise #1: Animating a Walk

In this exercise, you are going to use an IK skeleton to animate a simple four-legged walk. The timing of a walk varies widely, depending on the animal—a mouse steps much more quickly than an elephant. In this exercise, one step is animated every 12 frames.

1. Start by positioning the back legs. Rotate the back hips and place the right back foot forward. Exactly how far forward depends on the animal; a creature with longer legs may step as far as halfway up the body.

continues

Exercise #1: continued

 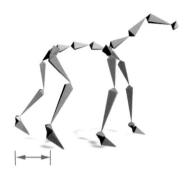

2. Position the front legs by mirroring the pose on the back legs, placing the left front foot forward. This means that, for this step, the forward feet (left front and right rear) remain planted.

3. Both pairs of legs should have the feet approximately the same distance apart. This distance is the stride length. Take a note of this distance as reference for the next step by estimating it or measuring it exactly.

4. Animate the first step. In a four-legged walk, you need to make sure both pairs of feet move the same distance. Move the time slider ahead to frame 12. Set keys for the feet that are currently forward. (right front and left rear.)

5. Rotate the shoulders and hips to mirror the pose on the first frame. Move them forward by the stride length. This causes the feet to lift off the ground.

6. Double the stride length to move the back feet forward, and then set a key. Scrubbing the animation produces a walk where the feet only slide.

7. Go to the middle of the stride (frame 6) and create the middle pose. Lift the two legs that are moving forward off the ground.

8. As in bipedal walk, lifting the legs throws the hips and shoulders out of balance slightly. Rotate the hips and shoulders so that the side with the moving leg is lower than the side with the planted leg.

9. Finally, the hips and shoulders also rise and fall vertically, much like a biped's hips. This is the key to implying the animal's weight. The recoil position, where the body absorbs the weight of the planted foot, is in this step at approximately frame 3. Move to that frame and lower both the hips and shoulders. At frame 6, they are at their peak. Move to that frame and lift the hips and shoulders so that the planted leg is at full extension.

10. Scrub the animation. This is just the first step. Repeat this procedure for each additional stride.

This gives you a basic walk. You might want to play with the timing of the feet, however, to get a little bit more realism in the walk. You can do this by offsetting the motion of opposite feet by a frame or two so that the feet don't hit at exactly the same time. Another trick is to add weight shifts for each step, which will help with the realism of the animation.

Other Four-Legged Gaits

In addition to normal walking, a four-legged animal usually has several different gaits. These are the walk, trot, canter, and gallop. The animal varies the timing and rhythm of its steps as it moves faster and faster.

Trot

The trot is a two-beat gait, seen quite often in horses. The animal's legs move in diagonal pairs, with the animal airborne for a few frames between each stride. Another way to view this is that, when the left front leg is fully back, the left rear is forward, and vice versa. During the trot, the animal holds its head higher than it does at the walk, and the head remains almost still along the vertical axis.

During a trot, the animal's legs move in diagonal pairs, with the animal airborne for a few frames between each stride.

Canter

The canter is a three-beat gait, with the legs generally working in the this sequence: left rear goes forward, right rear and left front move forward together, and finally the right front moves forward. At this last stage, after the animal uses the right front to push off for the next stride, there is a period where all four feet are off the ground. This gait also causes the animal's body to rock back and forth as it moves.

The canter is a three-beat gait. This sequence shows one half of the gait.

Gallop

The gallop is where the animal extends to its full reach and speed. The step sequence of a gallop is exactly the same as a canter, just faster and more stretched out. The horse is in the air longer because there's a bigger launch and the footsteps fall faster. This gives the impression of the feet moving in unison, but it's still three beats, as in the canter.

The gallop is where the animal extends to its full reach and speed. The step sequence of a gallop is exactly the same as a canter, just faster and more stretched out.

Stylized Walks

Another way to view a four-legged walk is in a more cartoony way. Think of the old vaudeville act where two guys get into a tattered old horse suit. In this case, the horse literally walks like two people stitched together. You animate the walk like a double two-legged walk. This forces you to have different joint constraints and body construction.

You can also stylize a four-legged walk by adding personality. Try to understand the character and his mood as you animate a walk. The mechanics of four-legged walks may be somewhat complex, but take the walk beyond mechanics. Even if the mechanics are not quite real, the audience will accept them as real if the resulting animation looks good.

The back legs on this dog are not realistic; they bend the same way human legs do. Still, the cartoon nature of his design permits us to do this and get away with it.

Reptiles

Quadrupedal reptiles, such as lizards and crocodiles, tend to keep their stomachs very close to the ground, with the legs splayed out to the side. With few exceptions, most four-legged reptiles have the same awkward position. This keeps the reptile's center of gravity quite low. This makes it more difficult to raise the body off the ground. As a contrast, quadrupedal mammals have their limbs directly underneath the body, which allows the legs to carry all the animal's weight, which is more efficient.

A reptilian walk is similar to a mammalian walk in that the front and back legs move in opposition. The reptile's low center of gravity, however, forces the body to work more. As it walks, a reptile bends its torso into a curve to help push the feet along. Despite this awkward motion, some reptiles are capable of moderate speeds. Crocodilians raise their bodies off the ground and make short, fast rushes. Short-bodied lizards also can move fast for short distances. In fact, some lizards can lift their front legs off the ground when running. Longer-bodied lizards have greater difficulty in raising their bodies, because they have short legs. This forces their bodies to move more like snakes do. In fact, if you reduce the legs completely, the result is a snake.

Crocodiles, as well as lizards and other reptiles, have legs that are splayed out to the side.

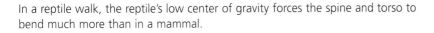

In a reptile walk, the reptile's low center of gravity forces the spine and torso to bend much more than in a mammal.

Snakes

Snakes move in a very unique way, and to the casual observer, it seems almost magical that an animal with no legs can move so quickly and gracefully. Snakes travel best on surfaces with obstructions and some roughness. This gives their bellies something to grip. Snakes do not do very well on slippery surfaces.

If you put a snake on loose sand, you can see that every part of its belly touches the ground, and it flows along in a series of S-curves. On the back of each curve, you can see that the sand has been pushed up. The body pivots and pushes sidewise against these piles and is propelled forward. It swims in water with the same motion.

Snakes have several different modes of locomotion. The method a snake uses depends on several factors, such as its size, the roughness of the surface, and the speed of travel. Typically, the snake finds a bump or a rough spot on the surface and pushes against that with its body to move forward.

Serpentine Locomotion

Serpentine locomotion uses the classic S-curve and is the most common method of travel used by snakes. In lateral undulation, waves of sideways bending are propagated along the body from head to tail. The snake's muscles are activated sequentially along the body, relaxing and contracting to form an "S" shape. As the snake progresses, each point along its body follows along the path established by the head and neck, like the cars of a train following the engine as it moves along the track.

Sidewinding

Sidewinding is used by many snakes to crawl on smooth or slippery surfaces. It is similar to lateral undulation in the pattern of bending, but differs in a few ways. First, the snake's body doesn't slide along the ground; instead it lifts part of the body while firmly setting down other parts. This allows the snake to get a better grip.

Next, the parts of the body that are not firmly planted on the ground lift up from the ground, causing the body to roll along the ground from neck to tail, forming a characteristic track.

Finally, because the snake repeatedly lifts parts of the body, it moves diagonally relative to the tracks it forms on the ground.

Serpentine locomotion is the most common method of travel used by snakes. Each point of the body follows along the S-shaped path established by the head and neck, much like the cars of a train following the track.

When animating this type of motion, the distance that the snake lifts its body off the ground is usually measured in fractions of an inch, which is practically negligible from the audience's viewpoint. For added effect, you can exaggerate this lift.

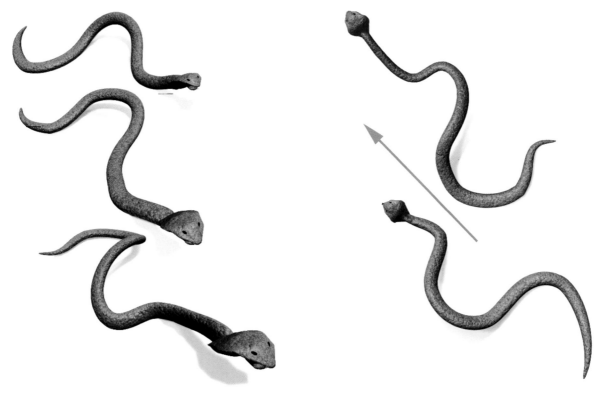

In sidewinding, the snake actually lifts parts of the body and sets them down again.

Sidewinding causes the snake to move diagonally relative to the "S" shape.

Concertina Locomotion

With concertina locomotion, the snake alternately bends up the body like an accordion and then lifts and straightens out the body to move forward. The front part of the body then comes to rest on the surface and the back part of the body is lifted and pulled up into the accordion shape again. Concertina locomotion is used mostly in crawling through tunnels or narrow passages and in climbing.

In concertina locomotion, the snake bends up the body like an accordion and then lifts and straightens out the body to move forward.

Rectilinear locomotion lets the snake move straight ahead with its body stretched out.

IK chains tend to favor a particular direction. If you build a chain that arcs to the left, getting it to bend to the right is usually either very difficult or impossible.

FK chains can also be problematic. With the bones linked in a simple hierarchy, moving one joint also moves all the children. This can be a real hassle when you want to animate smooth, undulating motions.

Rectilinear Locomotion

Rectilinear locomotion lets the snake move straight ahead with its body stretched out, or perhaps on a wide arc. This type of motion is used primarily by large snakes, such as boas and pythons. In rectilinear locomotion, the action is somewhat like rippling the belly, as the snake's belly scales are pulled forward and lifted off the ground, and then set down and pushed backward. Because the scales are aligned much like a ratchet, this pulls the snake forward.

Setting Up a Snake

The preceding sections covered the motions that snakes use to travel forward, but snakes can also perform many other motions. They can coil up and strike, climb trees, swim, and many other amazing things. In all these, the snake uses its entire body to move and position itself.

To animate a snake properly, you need to create a skeleton or other setup that provides maximum flexibility for the animator.

Your first instinct might be to create a simple chain of bones and link them together to form an IK or FK chain. This might work for a simple motion, but it has a number of drawbacks.

With standard IK and FK solutions seriously deficient for snake animation, you probably need to turn to other methods. One method may be to create a collection of skeletal bones that are not linked in a hierarchy. You would animate the snake by moving each bone individually. This, however, can be hard to manage.

Splines are a great method for animating snakes. A simple spline looks like a snake, and can be used for animation as well. Most packages support spline deformation in one form or another. Many packages allow you to animate the control points of the spline directly. If this isn't the case, you can make these points into one-point clusters and animate those.

Spline deformation, also known as a *wire deformer*, is probably the easiest tool for creating such a setup. In this method, an object's deformation is controlled by a separate spline. You can also use a tool such as a loft to build the snake, using a series of circular outlines to define the snake's diameter and a spline path to define the length. Most packages allow you to use this path as a control object as well, so animating this spline deforms the body.

Both these methods have one problem in that they don't preserve the volume of the snake's body. If you accidentally move two control points too far apart, the snake appears to stretch unnaturally.

Many software packages now support a tool that is generically dubbed *spline IK*, which uses a spline to control a chain of bones. The spline manipulates a chain of bones that, in turn, deform the model. This is by far the best solution to animate an animal such as a snake. The spline allows for easy manipulation, whereas the bones keep the creature's body from gaining or losing volume.

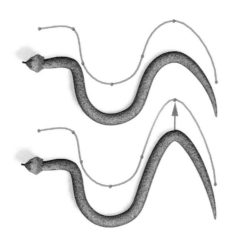

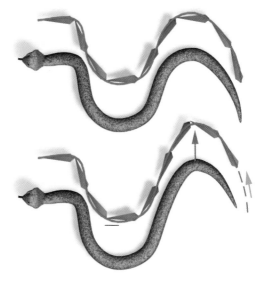

A spline manipulates a snake efficiently, but it is very easy to stretch the snake unnaturally.

Spline IK is perfect for snakes. The spline controls the shape of the IK chain, the bones of which deform the snake while they keep its volume constant.

The head of the snake definitely moves differently from the rest of the body. You need to set up the snake with a short "neck" area to allow the head to move independently. This way the snake can lift its head and look around, for example. This can be a separate chain of bones, or you can manipulate the controlling spline as well.

Dinosaurs

Dinosaurs are a unique case because we do not have much direct reference as to how they moved. There are no videotapes or films of these creatures in their natural habitat. Many scientists have tried to decipher dinosaur locomotion from the fossil record, but their conclusions are always open to debate. Observations of similar animals that are still living give us the best motion reference. Four-legged dinosaurs, such as a triceratops, would most likely have moved like a large four-legged modern animal, such as a hippo or rhinoceros.

Bipedal dinosaurs, such as a T-rex, are a bit more difficult to pin down, because no creatures alive today have a similar body. To figure out how these creatures moved, scientists have tried to reconstruct the walks and runs using sophisticated physical models. Movies such as *Jurassic Park* have popularized one particular brand of locomotion, which is based, to some degree, on the scientific research into this subject. This style seems to make a lot of sense and is the one we will use.

The back legs of a two-legged dinosaur are much like those of a bird. The dinosaur walks on his toes, with the body generally upright. The long tail acts as a counterbalance, which allows the upper body to pivot at the hips freely. As the dinosaur walks, the hips pivot much as a human's do, but the tail also rotates a bit to compensate.

As a bipedal dinosaur begins to run, the shoulders drop significantly as the body stretches out. This allows the tail to stretch out and counterbalance the upper body, which makes the locomotion process more efficient.

How did two-legged dinosaurs move? Because there are no dinosaurs alive today, we can only speculate.

One theory is that dinosaurs moved somewhat like birds. As a bipedal dinosaur began to run, the shoulders dropped significantly as the body stretched out to maintain balance.

Insects and Spiders

Insects and spiders are fairly easy to animate. Because an insect is the quintessential segmented creature, its parts can be built separately and connected together via a simple hierarchy. Shape animation or skeletal deformations are not needed for such a creature, because an insect's exoskeleton does not change shape. The one exception may be antennae on the insect, which can be animated with bones, or more directly, using a simple bend modifier.

Insects and spiders don't need to be deformed like animals with skin.

This spider is built of simple segments.

Setting Up Insects for Animation

Even though your insects may not need to be deformed, it can be a good idea to use IK chains for the legs. An insect's legs are typically composed of three joints connected to the underside of the body. These three joints are the insect equivalent of our thigh, shin, and foot.

An IK chain is used to manipulate the legs.

A simple three-joint IK chain for each leg makes animation much easier, because the only objects that need to be animated are the insect's feet and body. Legs can be built with the joints as separate segments. These can then be linked to the IK chains so animation can take place. You can also build the legs as a single mesh, which then must be deformed.

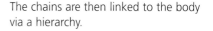

The chains are then linked to the body via a hierarchy.

Analysis of Six-Legged Walks

If four-legged walks seem complex, then six legs might seem intolerably difficult. This, fortunately, is not the case. An insect walk actually follows a definite, repeatable pattern that can be animated fairly easily. A six-legged walk is very similar to the four-legged walk: the front two legs simply take a step forward with one foot, and then the other. The second set of legs mirror this motion. The insect's third set of legs simply mirror the second again, closely matching the motion of the front legs, just offset slightly. Generally, insects keep at least three legs on the ground, forming a stable tripod at all times.

Animating the walk of an insect is simply a matter of getting the front legs to walk, mirroring this motion on the second set of legs, and then mirroring the motion of the second set of legs on the third. The legs of an insect have three main segments, with the first segment, closest to the body, acting like a suspension bridge that holds the body of the bug aloft.

Insect legs suspend the insect's body like a bridge.

Moving the Body

Like the body of a two- or four-legged creature, the body of an insect bounces up and down as the creature walks. This rate of bounce is directly proportional to the rate of the walk. The body bounces up and down once per step—meaning the insect bounces twice for a full cycle of right and left leg steps. The bug is highest when the legs are in the middle of the stride.

The rate of an insect walk depends on the species of bug and the bug's demeanor. Generally, bugs move pretty fast compared to mammals, and a quarter or eighth of a second per step is not out of the question. When walks get this fast, the frame rate of the animation becomes a limiting factor. At 24fps, an eighth second stride takes only three frames per step. This is about as fast as a walk can be animated, with one frame each for the forward, middle, and back portions of the step. This animation, at six frames per step, gives you a good pace for the insect walk.

1. At frame 0, the insect is at the bottom of the stride. Move the abdomen down vertically.

2. At frame 6, the insect is at the top of its stride. Move the abdomen up vertically.

3. At frame 12, the cycle repeats. Copy the abdomen position key from frame 0 to this frame.

4. To get enough up and down motion for a full cycle of steps, copy these keys again to make a second cycle, for a total of 24 frames.

Moving the Legs

The legs are best dealt with a set at a time. The front legs are always a good guide, so these are best animated first. Once the front legs are moving, the rear sets of legs can be keyframed in the same manner.

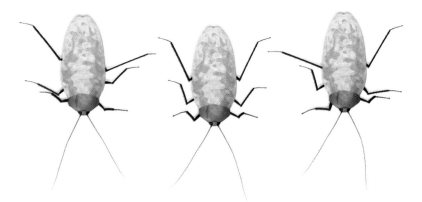

The extremes of an insect walk. When the right leg is forward the left is back and vice versa. Notice how each set of legs mirrors the position of the one in front of it.

Front Legs

The following steps show you how to move the front legs:

1. At Frame 0, the right front leg should be rotated forward about 15 degrees, with the left front leg rotated back approximately the same amount. Both legs should be touching the ground.

2. At Frame 6, both legs should be roughly centered. The left front leg is moving forward, so it should be raised off the ground. The right front leg is firmly planted. The body at this point is also at its highest point.

3. At Frame 12, the legs switch—the left leg plants and the right leg lifts. The left front leg should be approximately 15 degrees forward, while the right front is 15 degrees back.

4. Repeat the same positions outlined in the previous steps for the opposite legs on frames 12 through 24. The left leg should be planted, while the right leg lifts and moves forward.

5. Scrub the animation and adjust the rotations of the front legs to make sure they remain planted on the ground throughout their respective steps.

Middle and Rear Legs

The middle and rear legs move in an identical manner to the front, but are mirrored. This makes creating the animation as simple as repeating the exact same steps as you did for the front legs—creating a key for the beginning, middle, and end of each step, and then adjusting the inbetweens as required.

One tactic to use with animating the rear legs is to copy and paste the animation from the front legs to the corresponding rear legs. For this to work, the pivots of all the joints of the respective legs need to be aligned along the same axis. If they are not, the rotations do not translate properly, and the legs can't mirror exactly the rotations of the front. To fix this, align all the pivots on the legs to the world axis before animation begins.

Another problem with copying the controllers may be one of scale. The cockroach, for example, has rear legs that are quite a bit longer than the front legs. Copied rotations from the front legs may not match up exactly. Copying controllers may serve as a good starting point, but the effectiveness of this tactic depends on the anatomy of the insect being animated.

Another factor to consider is timing. If all three legs in motion were to lift on the exact same frame, the animation would look stiff and unnatural. To compensate for this, slide the keys for each set of legs back a frame or two so that they each lift slightly behind the leading legs. This adds another extra touch of realism.

One final thing to consider with insects is their antennae. These act as feelers for the insect, constantly searching out a path for the bug to follow. Antennae can be animated using a number of methods, such as bones with a mesh deformation system. A simple bend modifier can also be quite effective, because the angle and direction of the bend can be keyframed to give a nice effect.

Spider Walks

An eight-legged walk is similar to a six-legged walk, with an extra set of legs to manage. Spiders can use the front legs for walking, in which case the fourth (rear) set of legs mirrors the rest.

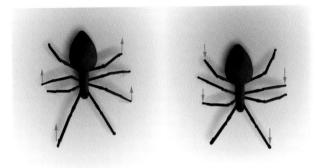

An eight-legged walk is similar to a six-legged walk, with an extra set of legs to manage.

Because a spider can easily support its body while walking on six legs, many times spiders use their front independently.

Because a spider can easily support its body while walking on six legs, many times they use their front independently. Similar to the way the insect uses its antennae to feel its way around, the spider may use its front legs to check out the road ahead. The spider can also use the front legs like arms to perform such tasks as spinning a web, or perhaps capturing dinner.

Conclusion

As you have seen, animals come in many sizes and shapes. Animating them does not need to be a complex task. Try to understand the way an animal moves through research and reference. Once you have the basics, you can filter those motions through the personality of the animal to turn it into a character.

CHAPTER 8

Anthropomorphic Animation

One of the most compelling reasons directors have for choosing digital character animation over other forms is the computer's capability to closely mimic reality. Not only has this capability given digital character animators some very nice jobs in Hollywood, but it also has taken Madison Avenue by storm. The capability to breathe life into a very realistic-looking product—such as a cereal box or ketchup bottle—gives 3D animation a leg up on the competition.

Breathing life into an otherwise inanimate object is known as *anthropomorphic animation*. It need not be restricted to advertising product shots; it has a number of uses. Think of the trees that sprang to life in *The Wizard of Oz*. If that film were done today, not only would Dorothy be hipper and more sarcastic, but those anthropomorphic trees would probably be digital. Animators have a long history of bringing inanimate objects to life—from Fleischer's cartoons of the 1930s to the present.

So how do you breathe life into something that doesn't have arms, limbs, or even a face? Through strong poses and good timing, which are the essence of good animation. Animating something as simple as a cereal box gives you good insight into the pure art of timing and motion that every animator should master.

How Real Can You Go?

One of the big questions you need to answer before designing or animating such a character is how real (or unreal) you want the character to be. Strictly put, any anthropomorphic character is not "real." By definition, anthropomorphism means bringing the inanimate to life, so any character you create is sure to include some degree of fantasy.

The answer lies in how far you want to take the fantasy. Perhaps the setting is a live-action horror flick where the chairs spring to life. Do the chairs move, but still retain their shape? Do the limbs of the chairs actually distort so that they resemble arms and legs? Do the backs of the chairs sprout faces? These decisions affect the tone and believability of the film.

The more fantastic you make the characters, the further away you get from reality. Still, a character out of fantasy might be the perfect solution for a given film. Most of these decisions are derived from the script and art direction of the film. In a commercial, the client also has a great deal of input. In your own film, you need to make the judgment call.

Creating Your Character

When working with an anthropomorphic character, modeling is always a consideration. Sometimes the task can be straightforward. How much time does it take to model a cereal box? Of course, if the cereal box sprouts a face, then the modeling task gets tougher.

As you create your character, you should also be figuring out who your character is and how to move it around convincingly. One method that might help is to determine what type of animal your character most resembles. With its four legs, a coffee table might be thought of as a dog, whereas a garden hose could be thought of as a snake. Like the classic flour sack, boxes lend themselves to bipedal motion, the bottom corners of the box being the feet and the top corners being the shoulders or hands.

In some cases, your character might be represented several different ways. A simple hot dog shape could be portrayed as snake or a worm. If you were to add limbs to the shape, you could very easily have a dog or a human-like character.

A simple hot dog. By how you create the character, you determine how it will move and act.

With a simple manipulation of the shape, the character becomes a snake.

Add lots more detail, and you get a human-like character.

Modeling Your Character

Once you've made some decisions about who your character is and how it moves, you need to model it. As with any character, you need to decide what geometry types to use—NURBs, polygons, and subdivision surfaces can all be employed. You also need to decide how much detail to add—whether your character has arms, legs, and a face.

Adding Faces

As you're well aware, most emotions can be portrayed through body posture alone, but if your character speaks, then the question of adding a face becomes important. You could add lips and a mouth, but this is the easy way out. If you're clever about these things, you can make your character speak without adding such artificial devices. The end of a vacuum cleaner's hose could be used as a mouth, for instance. Just by flapping a can's lid up and down, you can create some surprisingly convincing lip sync.

There is a lot more to this than just sticking a mouth on a character. Design is also part of the equation. The facial apparatus you choose and how clever it is reinforces what you are trying to say about the character or product. By highlighting the body structure of the object through the placement of a face, you can reinforce who the character is and how it is perceived. A character with a big mouth, for example, is typically more gregarious than one with a puny mouth.

If you do decide to give your character a face, then you can employ several methods. An integrated face has the elements built in to the surface of the character. This means a lot of modeling to get the face correct, plus extra modeling for the various morph targets. Alternatively, modeling a separate mouth or employing replacement mouths gives a more stylized look.

This can speaks by flapping its lid.

For a more stylized look, you can add a paste-on set of mouths.

You can also build the mouth into the surface of the can.

Adding Limbs

Another question concerns whether to give your character arms and legs. Your character may need arms if it is to pick up objects, for example.

This cola can has arms and legs, but are they really necessary? Sometimes, it's more challenging to go without such artificial devices and animate the shape itself.

This character has arms, legs, and a face. By the time your character looks like this, you can probably animate it as you would any other two-legged creature.

Of course, once your character has arms, legs, and a face, the animation task becomes pretty much the same as for any other human or animal character. Because these types of characters are covered elsewhere, this chapter focuses more on the characters that lack these additions.

Exercise #1: Designing an Anthropomorphic Character

Pick an ordinary object and design a character around it. Before you begin, visualize the personality of the character. If you can, try to use the shape of the object as a rough guide or perhaps picture it as an animal. Once you have a solid idea who the character is, model it.

Character Setup

Because just about any object can be an anthropomorphic character, setup varies widely between different characters. How your character is rigged depends on the tasks your anthropomorphic character needs to perform. Some characters are jointed, and animating them involves nothing more than moving and rotating the joints. A classic example is Luxo Jr, directed by John Lasseter at Pixar. In this film a simple jointed table lamp springs to life.

A character without joints needs to be deformed. You can deform a simple character, such as a box, through the use of a lattice, or perhaps other global deformers, such as bends, twists, and tapers. The box is very similar to the classic flour sack and can be set up using a skeleton in a similar manner.

More complex characters need more complex skeletons. If your character has appendages, such as the branches of a tree, these can be set up in much the same way as other characters with arms or legs.

Animating Objects

Animating a faceless, limbless object can be difficult, but it is also one of the best exercises an animator can undertake. Any emotions or attitude you bring out of a character are directly related to the timing and poses you give the character. Animating this type of creature can be fun because you're not encumbered by the expression on the character's face, the positions of the fingers, or whether the feet are placed realistically. The poses are typically broad and easy to create. The big secret in this type of animation is the timing.

The Big Secret: Timing

If you nail the timing and use lots of anticipation and overshoot, you should be fine. Really, the basic animation tools of squash and stretch, anticipation, overshoot, and moving holds are the only things you have in your animation arsenal. Because the character doesn't have such things as eyes or hands for the viewers to watch, they focus on the character, its poses, and the timing. Any timing glitches are more noticeable, and bad timing turns into *really* bad timing.

The size of your character determines to some degree how it moves, as well. Silverware sprung to life should move much faster, relatively speaking, than an anthropomorphic Chrysler Building. A character's personality also plays a factor. A dim-witted character moves more slowly than a bright and alert character.

Animating a Jointed Character

When you animate a jointed character, the tendency is to keep the joints rigid, with little or no deformation. You have to find the essence of the character in anticipation, overshoot, and moving holds. You also have to determine which parts of the object represent the body, the head, and the other parts found on a living being. For example, imagine the classic Pixar desk lamp that comes to life. The light source can be considered the face, and the reflector can be thought of as the head. The body continues down to the base.

Exercise #2: Animating a Static-Shaped Robot Arm

This exercise is a good one to help you understand how to animate a static-shaped, jointed character. It uses a simple robot arm. By rotating the joints, you can bring this object to life. You have the robot's arm notice a sphere, examine it, pick it up, and toss it off the screen.

This robot's arm is a nice example of a jointed, static-shaped character.

The arm can be set up two ways: either through forward or inverse kinematics (or both, if your software supports them). If you decide to use forward kinematics, then the joints can be linked together in a hierarchy. Those who decide to use inverse kinematics need to build a simple skeleton, linking the robot's arm joints to the bones.

The following are a few pointers to guide you in creating this animation.

Think of this joint as your character's waist. It enables your robot arm to bend over or stand up, so to speak.

Think of this joint as your character's head. By rotating it, your robot can shake its head yes and no and observe the ball.

continues

Exercise #2: continued

The claws can be thought of as a mouth. Much like a dog carries things in its mouth, your robot arm can pick up the ball in its "mouth."

The robot can also rotate at its base, turn around, or wag its "tail."

Animating Deformed Characters

Deforming a character as it bends and moves breaks the wall of ultra-realism, but the technique can give your character lots of personality. More variables exist in this type of animation than with static-shaped characters, so your options are numerous.

Just how you change your character's shape depends on the features and capabilities of your animation software. Not every package has every tool, so use the ones you have to the best advantage. Sometimes, creating a novel solution with a limited toolkit can be just the ticket to a great animation. As with any setup, keep it simple and straightforward. It is always best to have a simple but rock-solid setup than to have a complex one that needs fixing during animation.

Using Simple Deformations: Scale, Bend, Twist, and Tapers

Sometimes simple is better. Simple shapes such as boxes lend themselves to simple animation methods. Every decent package that I am familiar with enables you to scale an object along any axis and animate the scaling. This animation method might be all you need to give your character squash and stretch and to create a convincing animation.

A normal cereal box.

The box squashed by scaling.

The box stretched through scaling.

Scaling can pose problems because you can easily lose volume and make your character look like it is shrinking and growing rather than squashing and stretching. For example, if you stretch a character along the y axis, then you should shrink it along the x and z axes to maintain its volume.

Other techniques, such as bends, twists, and tapers, can give a more dynamic flair to your character by making it appear to be very flexible. If you're animating a simple box, you need to give it enough detail so that it deforms smoothly without showing the underlying structure. If you build it with NURBs or use subdivision surfaces, you can get away with a few subdivisions; however, a polygon-based box requires more.

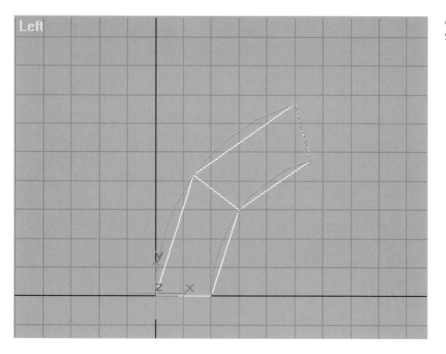

A polygonal box illustrates the need for subdivisions.

The more subdivisions the box has…

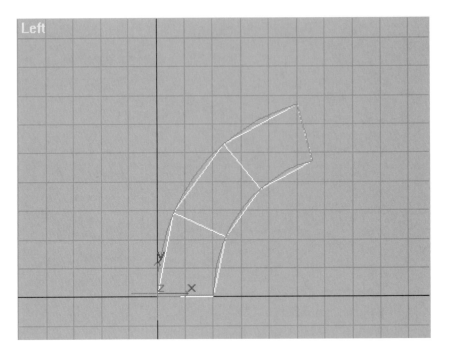

…the smoother it bends.

If you use patches or subdivision surfaces, you can get away with less detail.

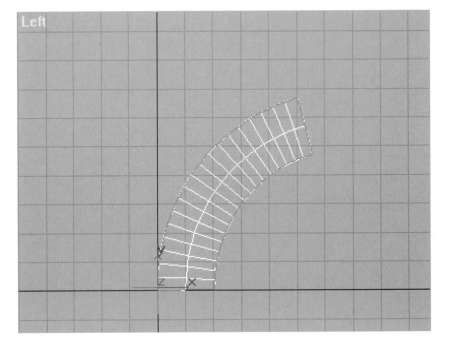

The bend modifier is great for giving the character a waist. Depending on the axis of the bend, the character can bend forward, backward, or from side to side.

Using a simple bend modifier, you can give a box a waist, and bend it forward...

...or backward.

Twisting a character is great for creating the illusion that it possesses hips and shoulders. In humans, the hips and shoulders twist back and forth during a walk, and this movement can be effectively simulated even in an animated box, if you use a twist. If the character needs to look over its right shoulder, twist the top half of its body around to the right.

A simple twist modifier enables your character to look to the left...

...or to the right.

Tapers are good for giving your character a feeling of weight and volume. Think of a character jumping and landing on the ground. You might want to scale the character as it hits the ground to give it a nice squash and a feeling of weight. By adding a bit of taper to the character, you can place more of that weight near the ground. The taper modifier is also good for cases where the character needs to stick out its chest.

Using a taper, you can push the character's volume around, and make it appear to do things such as stick its chest out...

...or bulge...

...or seem surprised.

Tools such as scale, bend, twist, and taper are quite handy, but they work best with simply shaped objects such as a cereal box or a television set. They do have their limitations; for instance, they can be imprecise when it comes to the exact placement of the feet. If you're trying to do a walk using only twists and bends, there's no real way to lock the feet to the ground. An alternative to such a walk might be a series of leaps or hops that don't depend on exact foot placement.

The following exercise illustrates how much personality you can get from a simple box by using nothing but timing and posing techniques.

Exercise #3: Animating a Box with Simple Deformations

First, you need to model a simple box the size and shape of a cereal box. Be sure to give the box enough detail so that it can twist and bend smoothly.

Place your box in the shot with the camera at a three-quarter view.

Next, use a deformation tool to twist the top of the box so it looks to the right. This motion should take about half a second. Be sure to anticipate this move with a small twist to the left for a few frames, and overshoot the pose by a few frames. Hold this pose for a half second with a moving hold.

Again, using anticipation and over-shoot, twist the box to the left so it looks over its shoulder. Make this turn a few frames faster than the first—about one-third of a second. After the box is looking over its left shoulder, add about a one-half-second moving hold to the pose.

Now twist the box back to the right, so it "looks" directly at the camera. Hold this pose for a few frames.

Now animate a strong anticipation, so that the box is leaning back and preparing to run out of the scene. It should take a third of a second to hit this pose. Hold the anticipation for a few frames with a moving hold.

Move the box off the screen by having it run, hop, or slide. Render a test, and then go back and tweak the animation until you are satisfied with it.

Using Lattice Deformations

Another easy method to shape and stretch characters is to use lattice deformations. With a minimum of fuss you can create nice, squishy deformations. To animate the character, you animate the lattice's vertices; the character's corresponding vertices follow along. If your object is too complex to be contained in a box, you can add multiple lattices, or they can take on more complex shapes if your software accommodates it. In fact, you can animate some very complex characters with lattices and lattice-like deformations.

Generally, you use lattices to reduce the number of vertices you need to control. Again, the theory of simplicity applies here. By moving one or two control points, you can completely reshape dozens of the object's vertices. Some people create a big problem for themselves by making their lattice nearly as complex as the model itself, which is self-defeating. The idea is to reduce the lattice to its simplest form to keep the animation easy. If you can get the effect you want by moving one point rather than ten, your job will be easier, and chances are that the animation will look smoother and more natural.

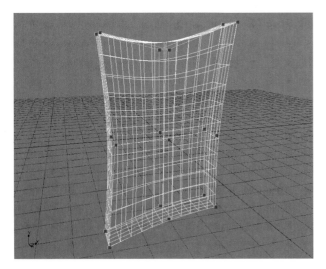

Keep your lattices as simple as possible.

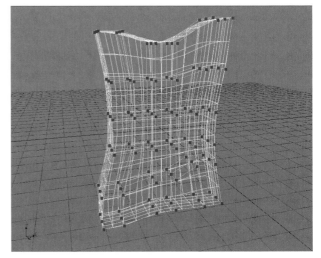

Too much detail in a lattice means more detail to move, which is self-defeating.

Bending Along a Spline

A good way to animate snake-like objects is to use a spline as a deformation tool. Use the spline as one axis of the character. When you bend and manipulate the controlling spline, your character follows. Controlling your character with a spline is as easy as controlling a few simple vertices.

Some packages have a tool that uses a spline to manipulate a skeleton. This is a great tool because the skeleton maintains volume in the character, while the spline makes manipulation super-easy.

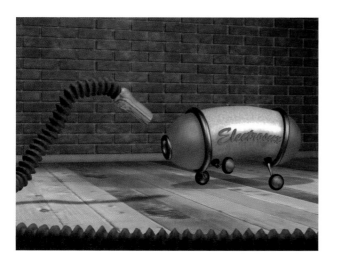

A spline can control snakelike objects, such as this vacuum hose.

Unfortunately, if you use a spline, you can very easily lose volume in the character.

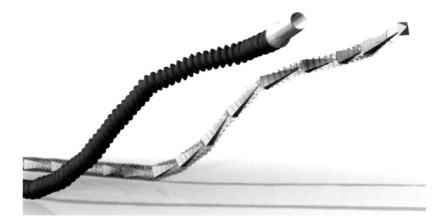

Spline-driven IK allows you to use a spline to control a skeleton, which makes maintaining volume much easier.

Using Skeletons

Skeletons are probably an animator's best tool for bringing inanimate objects to life. With them, even the simplest of objects can be given plenty of motion. Again, for most situations, it's best to keep the skeletons simple. For a box, you could use as few as four bones (one for each corner), though eight would be more practical, because you could place two bones on each corner and connect them to give your box knees and elbows. Bones are great because you can apply IK to them, which makes posing very easy and enables you to lock the feet in place during walk cycles.

digital character animation 2, volume II

A skeleton for a simple slice of Swiss cheese.

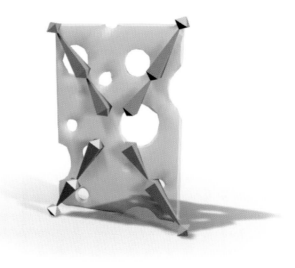

Exercise #4: Animating Ham and Cheese

Because they are rectangular, slices of ham and cheese are very similar to the box you just animated. However, this time you will use a skeleton to deform the character. The animation in this exercise is also more complex, because you will be animating two characters who interact with each other.

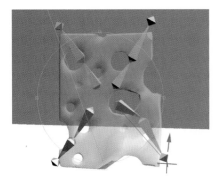

First, you need to construct a skeleton. You can set up the skeleton for use with IK. It is pretty much the same as a standard leg setup for a human character: the legs are IK chains that are hierarchically connected to the "body" at the hips.

Because the characters are so simple, you might not even need IK. Breaking the hierarchy at the hips gives you two free bones for the legs. The body simply "floats" above the tops of the legs.

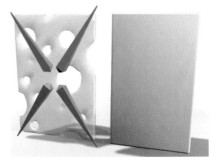

For experience with both methods, perhaps set up one character with IK and one without.

Now you need to make the characters interact to create a simple scene. First, you need to come up with some characterization, a little motivation, and a dash of conflict. Perhaps the ham is a shy suitor to the popular and rather gregarious cheese. He wants to ask her to dance, but he is too shy. This is certainly not the only story; you could swap the personalities and make the cheese a shy wallflower and the ham a bold suitor. If you want, you can also add a simple prop or two to help with the conflict—perhaps the two need to share a slice of bread.

However you complete this exercise, be sure to pay attention to characterization, staging, and the interactions between the characters.

The following is a more advanced exercise in that it uses slightly more complex characters.

Exercise #5: Bringing a Vacuum to Life

Again, you will be animating two characters: a vacuum cleaner and a hose.

The vacuum has four caster-like wheels. You need to make a decision about how to animate this character. Do the wheels simply roll? That would be the easiest to animate. Alternatively, the wheels can be thought of as the feet of a four-legged animal. In this case, they would step rather than roll.

How does a vacuum move? Does it roll around on its casters?

Or do the casters become "feet" that make it behave more like a four-legged animal?

continues

Exercise #5: continued

If you decide to make the casters roll, the setup is fairly straightforward. Using the casters as feet is more complex, so take a look at the next few steps to see how that is done.

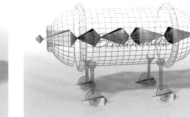

Much like the skeleton of a four-legged creature, the skeleton is centered around a "spine" that runs through the body.

Because the casters are on stems that detach them from the body, I find it easiest to use a broken hier-archy on the feet. I place a bone at each foot and use that as part of the deformation. The bones are not linked to the body.

This makes it easy to lock down the feet, but the body does float "free" above the feet. Pay attention to the body to make sure it is in a natural position.

The hose is pretty much the same animal as a snake. Setup is similar.

The easiest way to set up the hose is to use a spline-based IK system.

For those without spline IK, forward kinematics is also an option.

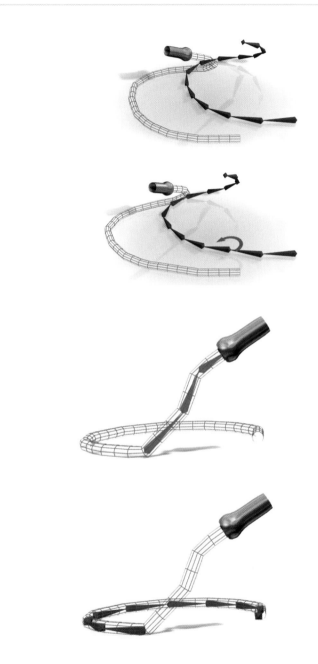

One problem with using a single chain is that it makes posing the "head" of the hose much harder. Here, manipulating a joint near the tail moves the head drastically. It is best to create two chains.

One short chain is centered around the "neck" of the hose. This way, you can pose the head much more quickly.

The rest of the body is manipulated by a longer chain that terminates at the neck.

As with the previous exercise, you need to figure out your characters, their motivations, and a conflict to create a simple scene. Perhaps the vacuum is a shy puppy who encounters a vicious snake (the hose). Whatever the story, be sure to pay attention to proper staging, acting, and characterization.

Conclusion

One of the most important things to remember about animating inanimate objects is to be true to the character. The type of object you're animating is very much a part of the character. A box of hot pepper animates differently than a box of oatmeal, even though they're the same shape. Just as in any other form of animation, be true to your character. If you understand your characters, everything else falls into place.

CHAPTER 9

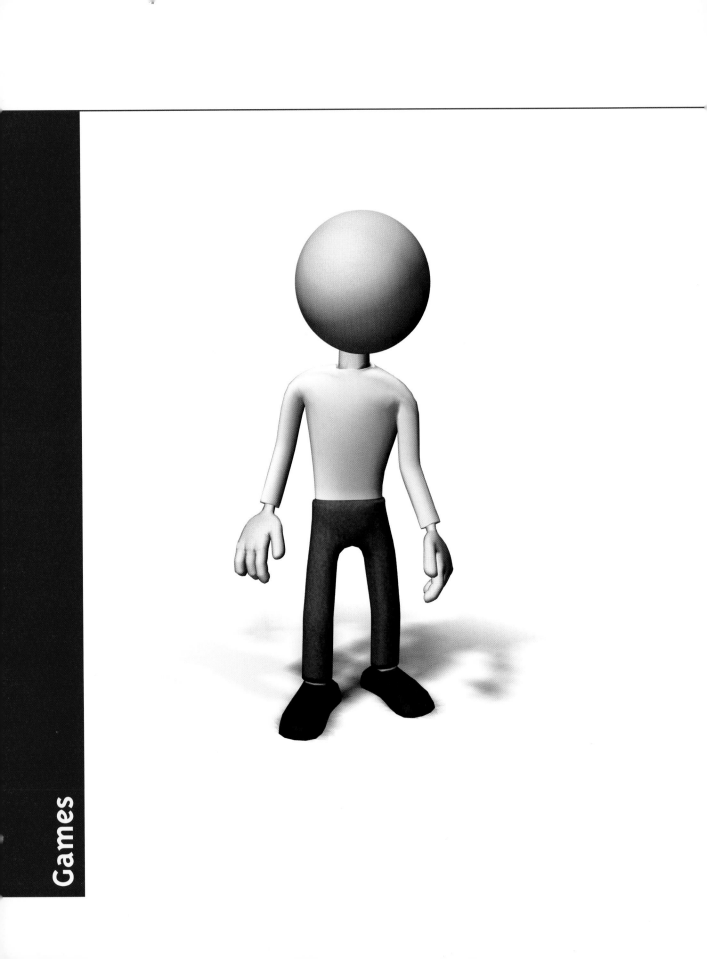

Games

Games are a billion-dollar industry and a big part of the animation business. Almost every game has animation in one form or another, and most of that animation is in 3D. Animating for a game is very much like animating for film or video, but with a few restrictions.

First of all, because games happen in real time, they place a huge demand on the console to render scenes in real time. To accommodate this, most characters have only limited detail. Deformations can also be difficult to compute in real time, so most games do not incorporate features such as dialogue with accurate lipsync. Lipsync and dialogue are also not used because most characters are so small you never see it. Finally, hard core gamers do not agree that it adds to game play.

Animating for a game console is an exercise in limitations. Each console has a fixed limit in terms of how much data can be in the scene at any given time. If you have a complex environment, the characters may need to be less complex. If you have a lot of characters, you may need to share animation cycles between them, for example. Knowing your platform and its limitations will allow you to budget your animation.

Despite the huge number of titles, most games fall into a few broad categories: driving, fighting, strategy, action adventure, and so on. Typically, the main character needs to overcome obstacles, fight off the bad guys, and get some sort of treasure or goal. Sounds a bit like standard storytelling, but the difference is that the player almost always has control of the main character.

Producing Games

Game production is very similar to other forms of animation production. A game, however, is a piece of software that lives on a CD, DVD, or a game cartridge. The fact that games are software makes creating them much more computer-intensive than creating images for film. Gameplay is controlled via a computer program that takes input from the player, usually via a joystick or game pad, and uses this input to direct the character through a virtual world. This makes creating a game much more like developing software than a movie, in that programmers are heavily involved and the game must be thoroughly tested to make sure it is as bug-free as possible before release.

People Involved in Game Production

There are a number of different jobs that need to be done when creating a game. On the creative side, there are the typical modelers, animators, texture mappers, and other artists. On the technical side are programmers. Producers, of course, are always needed to make sure the job gets done.

Game Designer. The game designer is the head creative person regarding the gameplay, much like the writer of a book or director of a film. The designer determines how the game will be played. Often, one of the game designer's big tasks is to create a design document, sometimes referred to as the *project bible*. This document details the game's technical specs, including gameplay, characters and settings (possibly including diagrams or drawings), level descriptions, maps of the virtual world, and so on.

Art Director. This is the person who decides how the game looks visually. Much like how a director brings a writer's vision to the screen, the art director brings the game designer's vision to the screen. The designer is usually a visual artist who works along with a number of other people, including producers and animation directors, to name a few.

Producers. Much like in film production, the producer is the project's manager. The producer must keep the entire team productive and the lines of communication open while making sure the project comes in on time and budget. Producers also continually work out budgets for future projects through what they learn from existing productions. The producer is the point person for the client interaction.

Programmers. Programmers create the software that is the game. They also control the interface and are the ones who connect the animation of the characters to the actions of the players.

Programmers come in many flavors. AI (artificial intelligence) programmers work closely with the game designer to determine how a game is played. There are also high-level (broad strokes) and low-level (micro code) programmers, as well as creature programmers who handle all of the character animation—working with AI. Too, there is always a lead programmer, who hopefully is a guru with some management skills. Finally, in games the technical directors are the powerhouse of programming, handling all kinds of important stuff like lighting, textures, and management of assets so the game console doesn't hit its limit. A programmer is a very creative individual, and has quite a bit of technical skill, but usually not much artistic skill. Sometimes, it's as though artists and programmers speak different languages, which can make communication difficult within the production. In this situation, a good producer can help keep the lines of communication open.

Artists. In addition to programmers, there are plenty of artists. Production designers, working with the art director, design the look of the game and the world. Modelers and texture artists create the characters and environments. The animators rig characters and deal with other animation-related technical issues, as well as bring the characters to life and also animate other aspects of the game. Artists in games, unlike those in film, wear many hats, and it is greatly encouraged to have a broad range of skills—from rigging characters to animating them.

Additional people. On a larger production, there may also be intermediate people. These may include specialized artists such as maquette sculptors and art wranglers, as well as leads, junior programmers, and artists. In addition, you will probably have voice talent, sound designers, composers, system administrators, and many other people involved with the production.

Platforms

The game platforms for which you design are always moving targets. It seems as though every year a new game platform appears on the scene that trumps last year's in terms of performance and features. A platform can be a standalone game console, such as the Playstation, or a general-purpose computer, such as a PC. Each platform is different, so the animation requirements for each are different as well.

Writing games for consoles is good in that the console has a fixed specification. If your game runs on one console, it runs on every console. You know exactly what the console can and cannot do, so you can maximize your game's performance. Developing for a specific console means that you need to purchase a development kit from the manufacturer as well as submit your game for approval. Licensing also factors into the equation, because most console manufacturers demand a cut of the action. Many studios develop for multiple platforms to try and make the game available to as many people as possible and maximize profits.

The problem with developing for multiple platforms is that it can double or triple the workload. The game is usually written for the most capable platform; then features are removed for the remaining platforms. Removing features and still making the game play can take up a lot of resources, sometimes as much as writing the game from scratch.

Writing a game for a personal computer avoids many of the development and licensing issues that are inherent to proprietary consoles. The fastest PCs are also usually faster than the fastest consoles. Still, most people don't have the fastest PC, so game developers wind up writing for the lowest common denominator, which can lessen the maximum performance of the game. Additionally, no two PCs are exactly alike, so testing is much more complex. Still, it is much easier to develop for the PC, and the audience for PC gaming historically demands more storytelling and not so much "twitch and bleed." This is good for animators because they get to exercise their storytelling skills. Historically, the frame rates for games were below those of film or video. As the game engines have gotten more horsepower, however, this line is blurring significantly, and many games are now animated at the maximum rate of a TV set (60 fields per second), meaning the animation updates on every field of interlaced video. Many character-driven games need a little more overhead for things such as deformations, so they run at 30 frames per second, which gives them twice as much time to update the scene before it hits the TV screen.

Game Design

Whereas an animated film has a script and a storyboard, the game has a design document that must be followed. The functional spec will determine the goals for each level and will state broad strokes describing the gameplay of each room and level. The overall design depends a lot on the platform as well as the type of game. There are many different game genres, which can determine how the characters are animated.

Creating Characters for Games

Creating a character for a game is similar to most other types of modeling. The memory limitations of the game platform, however, place a fixed constraint on the amount of geometry and the number of textures that can be used at any one time.

The game designer, production designer, and art director usually design or manage the design of the main characters for the game. This design process is much like that for film, in that it involves many conceptual drawings and perhaps even a clay sculpture. Many times, this design is more complex than the game engine allows, so it is up to the modeling and texture artists to realize this vision as closely as possible while still keeping the models animatable.

Low-Poly Modeling

This is, by far, the most popular way to build characters for gaming. The methods are pretty much the same for subdivision surface modeling, except that the poly count should be kept down, and so the surface is not subdivided.

Typically, each character is budgeted a fixed number of polygons, which should be outlined in the design document. The more characters and props you have in the scene, the lower the per-character budget. Usually characters are limited to somewhere around 2,000–4,000 polygons, sometimes less. This can vary widely, depending on the game platform. Sometimes, you can have up to four levels of detail on a character, where the lowest would be to a few hundred polygons, but that low level of detail is for a character that would never be any larger than 50 pixels, such as a pedestrian in a driving game.

A low-poly character for a game.

Textures

Because most game engines are limited on the amount of geometry they can handle, much of the detail for a character must reside in the texture. A good texture map can provide lots of detail and make a character seem much more complex than it really is. However, texture memory is still fixed on game consoles, just as geometry memory is. This limits the resolution of the textures and forces the production to budget textures. For example, on the Playstation 2, a texture is limited to 128×128 pixels, and a character can have only a few of these. To budget textures, some productions use compression or reduce the color palette.

The medals, buttons, and necktie on this character are all modeled out of geometry, which takes up too much room in a game engine.

Instead, create the objects as textures.

When rendered in the game engine, the results are almost identical, but use significantly less geometry.

Once the character is modeled and textured, it's a very good idea to view your model inside your game environment as soon as you possibly can. This keeps you from running into scale, texture, polygon count, and design issues late in the production process, when they're much harder to fix.

Setup for Games

Rigging a character for a game is very similar to other types of rigging, and depends on how the characters are animated. It used to be that games were created with only segmented characters. Deforming a mesh in real time was too difficult. This has changed, however, and most game engines support deformations of some form or another, which allows for single-skin character modeling. Skeletal deformation does take a bit of computing power, so a segmented character might be more efficient, though it usually won't look as good. Most game consoles can handle weighted vertex skinning, if the programmers know how to write it. This makes the skinning look much better than segmented characters.

Most game engines now support skeletal deformations, which allow for single-skin characters such as this.

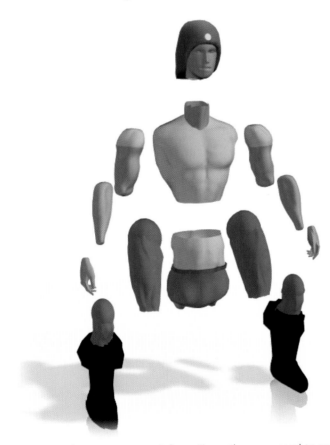

If your engine does not support deformations, then you need to segment your characters.

In either event, you are likely to want to use a skeleton to control the character. This can be set up pretty much to your liking. Typically the joint rotations are all that are translated to the game. Some companies, however, build their own IK solvers into their proprietary game engines. Some programmers also set limits on how the characters should be built. In either case, you might have set parameters for building the skeleton, particularly if any IK solutions are going to be used real-time in the game. Most games do not yet contain much facial animation and lipsync. This is mostly a design decision, as most characters in games are photographed full body, which minimizes the facial area. In addition, most hard-core gamers are more concerned with action over dialogue.

For those who need to perform facial animation or other types of deformation, morph targets are the best option, simply because they're computationally lighter than bones. Some games even use morphs for animation of hands. Again, many of the technical issues are dictated by the game engine and the programmers.

As with film, don't start adding the skeleton until the game designer approves the model. You should also be sure that the animator's skeleton is the same as the one the programmer uses. If the two are not identical, then your animation looks wrong when it is converted to the game engine. Many times the programmer needs a copy of the skeleton saved out with all rotations "zero-ed out" so that the skeleton is in its most neutral position to accept the animation data for the game.

One more important item to test is how the character moves in the game engine. Once you finish your skeleton, do a test animation where the character makes some very precise and predictable moves. For example, move the knee from zero to ninety degrees over the course of 10 frames. If your conversion software is correct, the animation in the game engine should match the animation in the 3D package exactly. If not, it needs to be fixed, usually by the programmer with a lot of help from the animator.

Animating for Games

Once you have a character rigged and tested, it is time to begin animation. Creating animation for games is fairly straightforward. The big difference is that outside of the cut scenes between game levels, you rarely animate anything straight through. All animation in a game is composed of short cycles and moves that are strung together to make continuous animation.

Test your character's motion in the game engine to make sure it matches your 3D package. If the knee moves 90 degrees in one, it should move 90 degrees in the other.

Games and Staging

As with film, characters in game animation still need to play to the camera. The camera, however, is usually under the control of the player. This can bring up some thorny issues. If the game is true 3D—not side scrolling—all moves must look good from all angles, making the job even more difficult than film. Most gamers demand gameplay where they can see the character in third person. Even the online first-person shooter games, such as Quake, see the other characters running around. Before you begin animating for a game, you need to understand where the camera is and how the audience is going to see your characters.

Games can be either first or third person. In a first-person game, the player sees everything in a POV perspective, which eliminates most animation of the main character. A third-person game shows you the character's motion in its entirety, which should be a lot more fun (and work) for the animators.

With a first-person camera, the player looks through the character's eyes.

A third-person camera includes the character.

If the game is shot in third person, you need to get some more information. How far away is the camera? If the player needs to see small, precise motions, you need to either bring the camera in close or animate the actions more broadly.

Another question is cutting. Does the camera move with the character all the time or do you use cinematic cutting?

The camera can follow the character by running along a rail locked to the character in an over-the-shoulder shot. This is very simplistic, but works well for single-player games. One problem is that you usually see the character from the back, which restricts animation of the main character.

With a "rail" camera, the camera that is linked to the character follows the character exactly. This works well for single-player games.

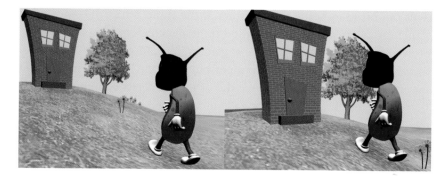

With a fixed camera, the character can move toward and away from the camera. This can also be good if more than one player is active.

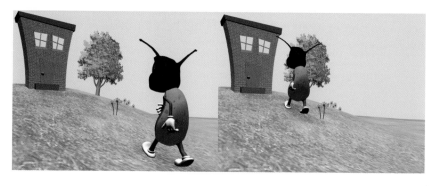

You can also have a camera that is controlled by the player and offers multiple views.

Another method is to use a stationary camera. This is good for scenes that are in smaller spaces, such as rooms or caves. For open spaces, you might want to free up the camera to give characters control over where they can look.

For games with multiple players, such as a sports game or fighting game, the camera may need to be more dynamic to include the action of both players. In a basketball game, the camera's position may be based on the position of the ball. In a martial arts duel, the camera needs to frame both characters.

Standard Moves

Most animation for games is done in short little segments, which are strung together as the game is played to give the illusion of continuous motion. Most games have a stock inventory of cycled motions that cover the basic needs of the game—running, jumping, standing, fighting, and so on.

Moves need to be short in order to preserve interactivity. If players move the joystick, they don't want to wait several seconds for an action to complete before the character responds. No matter how good it looks, the gamers of the world will loathe your animation if it takes too long to play back and spoils their control of the character.

Here are the basic moves for most characters in a game:

> **Idle.** The idle is the motion that the character does when the player is not using the joystick. The character is typically standing in a moving hold. There might be a shift of weight, breathing, scratching, looking around, and so on. These motions should be cycled over approximately 30–40 frames.

> **Run.** In most games, the character always seems to be in a hurry to get somewhere or get away from some threat. The run is very much a staple of gaming, and almost every game has a run cycle, usually about 18 or fewer frames. Also, sometimes there is a jog and a sprint version of a run.

> **Walk.** For those times when a character is not running, you need a walk. This is usually about 24 or fewer frames. Also, there sometimes is a need for a crouching walk, a injured walk, and so on.

Other locomotion. Depending on the game, you might also need other gaits, such as a sneak, somersault, leap, crawl, or a skip. Most of these are 24 or fewer frames.

React. For added realism, it's a good idea to animate your character reacting to something. This reaction could be anything from a head turn to a full-body take. The reaction is dependent upon what is interacting with the character, such as react to bite, react to shot, react to fire, etc. This is usually about 15 or fewer frames.

Death. If your character gets shot, stabbed, shocked, or clobbered with a mallet, it needs to die. Death can take many forms, and a single game is likely to have several ways for your character to die. This usually isn't a cycle and takes 15 or fewer frames.

Knockdown. Those times where your character gets hit but doesn't die, it may be knocked on its face or rear end. This motion is typically used in fighting games, is not cycled, and takes 12 or fewer frames.

Get up. If a character reacts to something and falls to the ground because of it, it needs to get up. The first frame of this motion should hook up with the last frame of the react motion. The last frame usually hooks up with the first frame of the idle motion. Getting up is usually about 30 or fewer frames.

Attack. A cycle of your character punching, kicking, clobbering, and so on. Each game has different requirements. In a fighting game, for instance, the attack move might be a kick or punch; a creature game might use a bite or claw; an armed game might use the aiming and firing of a weapon, as follows:

Aim: usually about 10 or fewer frames

Shoot: usually about 14 or fewer frames

Bite: usually about 14 or fewer frames

Punch: usually about 14 or fewer frames

Kick: usually about 14 or fewer frames

All these frame counts are obviously dependent upon the console you are developing for and the programmers involved, the game engine, and so on.

Turn. This is a very important move, as it allows your character to change directions. You may need to create several turns—a running turn, a walking turn, and so on. This move is usually more than 10–12 frames.

Other moves. Of course, characters in games may need to open doors, climb ladders, drive cars, swim, and fly, among many, many other types of motion. Each game is different and requires many of its own custom motions.

Cycles

Many of these standard motions, such as the runs and walks, are cycled motions. Much of the screen time for your characters is spent in cycles. Learning how to make a cycle that doesn't look like a cycle is an essential skill.

Creating a Cycle

A cycle for a game is fairly easy to create, and a bit more difficult to get perfect. The key is to duplicate the first frame of the cycle to the frame after the end of the cycle to make sure everything syncs up. After that, the various motions of the character are offset so their cycles don't all repeat on the same frame. This makes your character look much more lifelike and natural. If parts of the body have cycles that terminate on the same frame, it will be very obvious and look mechanical within the paltry 24 or so frames you have for the cycle.

Most cycles are animated as though the character is walking on a treadmill. This means that the feet are not locked to a fixed point in space as with most walks. Instead, the feet slide along the floor at a constant rate. This rate also determines how fast the character moves through the game, which should be communicated to the programmer.

Animating a Simple Cycled Walk

By now, you should be fairly familiar with the mechanics of a simple walk. Key to a cycle is getting the motions to overlap naturally and still sync up when the motion loops. This walk is animated using an IK skeleton.

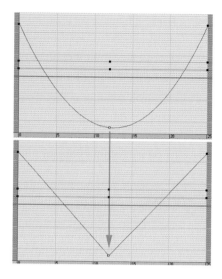

1. It's best to start with a pose that has the feet furthest apart. Start with the right foot forward. Determine the length of the cycle, in frames. The cycle covers two steps. This cycle is 24 frames. Copy the pose on the first frame to frame 25.

2. Go to frame 12, halfway through the cycle. Move the right foot all the way back to mirror the pose from frame 1.

3. Adjust the curve for the right foot from frames 1–12. It should move linearly from front to back, which keeps the foot moving at a constant rate. Do the same for the left foot from frames 13–25. The character now looks as if it is skating.

4. Once the feet are moving linearly, you can now work on the rest of the walk. First, get the hips moving. As you remember, the hips bounce up and down as well as counter-rotate as the legs move. At this point, it is probably best to animate these on the beat, so that the hips are highest at frames 6 and 18.

5. Next, animate the feet and legs of the passing position. Use the hip motion as a guide.

6. Finally, animate the twist of the spine and the swing of the arms to oppose that of the hips and legs. Again, stick to the beat of the walk; you can adjust the timing later.

7. As you animate all these moves, remember that the start and end poses need to be identical. If you modified one or the other, you need to copy keyframes to make sure they sync up.

8. Set your animation package to loop and play the walk. The motions should match up over the loop. If not, try to use the first and last keyframe to your advantage. Let the software inbetween the last few frames of the cycle to get a smooth loop.

The smooth loop just created certainly works, but all the moves were animated on the beat, so the cycle looks mechanical and stale. You need to adjust the individual joints so that the cycles overlap naturally.

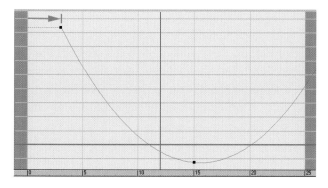

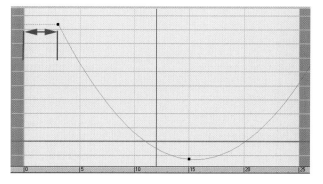

9. Start with the arms, which usually drag behind the legs by a few frames. Move these keys back by three frames. Play the cycle.

10. You may notice that the arms go dead for the first three frames of the cycle. This happens because the start pose was moved forward, creating a flat spot in the curve.

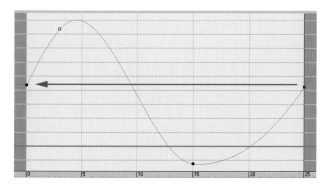

11. To compensate for this, go to frame 25 and set keys for the arms. Copy these keys to frame 1 so the cycle matches up.

12. Continue to adjust the offsets in the same manner for the rest of the body.

13. When you're finally satisfied with your results, render frames 1 through 24. Frame 25 is not rendered, because it was used simply to help the cycle loop properly.

Moving Characters

Because cycles are essentially the digital equivalent of walking on a treadmill, the way to move the character forward as it walks is to translate the master node of the skeleton. This work is usually the job of the programmer who connects the action of the game pad to the action of the character. Sometimes the programmer will ask the animator for a linear curve of translation that moves the character through space along with the cycle. For the character to look good while it is running and walking, the programmer needs to know the stride length of the character (the distance the character moves forward with each step). Most programmers are able to use a formula to figure out this stride length and calculate the distance of the gait.

Working with stride length alone may be problematic if the character moves at variable speeds based on the position of the joystick. In this case, the feet may have to slide a bit. One solution may be to have walks and runs that move at different speeds. As the character accelerates, it goes from a walk to a run to a fast run. This puts more burden on the animators and programmers, but it looks better than feet that slide.

Hooking Up

Getting from one cycle to another can be problematic. It is a good idea to make the transitions as easy as possible by standardizing your motions. When doing walks and runs, it is a good idea to always start and end each cycle on the same foot and facing the same direction. This way, the transition between the walk and the run is much easier. Moves such as attacks should be able to hook up with other motions as well. It is a good idea to start these on the same foot in much the same manner as walks and runs. Most programmers will ask all moves that are not cycles to begin at the idle/stand pose and return to that pose.

To make the game as interactive as possible, it may be necessary to break out of a cycle in the middle to substitute a new action. This task may fall on the programmer, who has to devise an algorithm to get the joints from point A to point B in a few frames. Typically, this sort of automatic inbetweening can look mechanical.

In lieu of this, you could also create short bridging motions that are only a few frames long. These can be substituted in between the cycles to make a smooth transition.

Flowcharting

In a complex game, a character may need to move between a few dozen motions. This can quickly create an agonizingly large number of bridging motions.

A more comprehensive way to view the myriad of combinations is to create a flowchart. This is something usually done by the game designer along with the creature programmers, and it can help animators understand all the motions and bridging motions they need to complete. There are several types of flowcharts.

One-to-One

This is the simplest type of motion. In this, a character goes from one move to the next in a linear fashion. This is very limiting, because the character cannot get from a stand to a run without first going through a walk.

One-to-one bridging takes a character from one move to the next in a linear fashion.

One-to-Many

One-to-many bridging uses a central pose, which is typically a neutral stand, as the central point from which all other motions branch. This type of bridging provides slightly deeper gameplay but is still very limiting for most games.

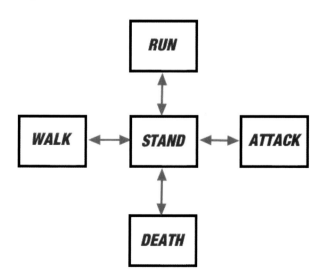

One-to-many bridging uses a central pose, typically a neutral stand, as the central point from which all other motions branch.

Many-to-Many

Many-to-many bridging is much better for most games. It allows for any move to be linked to another. Of course, this can get very complex if all moves are bridged to all other moves. However, it is usually not necessary to do so. For example, a character does not die unless it is attacked, so having a bridge from a simple walk to death is never needed. The best idea is to arrange the flowchart hierarchically, starting with a neutral motion such as standing.

Many-to-many bridging is much better than other bridging methods for most games. You can choose to link any move to any other.

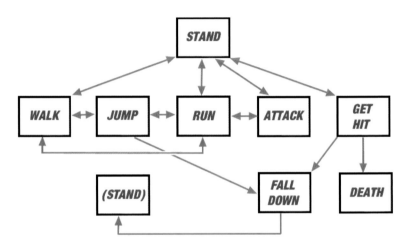

You also need to create bridging motions, where the last frame of one motion is bridged to the first frame of another. A run transitioning to a jump usually needs a bridging motion, for example. Usually these motions are only a few frames long. Stand to a walk might also need a bridging motion that anticipates the first step. This motion might also get double use to start a run, saving you a bit of animation time.

Some moves may not need bridging motions. If the walk and run cycles start on the same foot, then you might be able to go directly from one to the other.

As you work through the flowchart, you need to write down all the motions that need to be animated, as well as all the bridging motions you need to transition between them.

Once you have the list of the required motions, you have a list of the animation needed for the game. In creating this animation, it is best to work in sections and get your approvals at every step, if for no other reason than to save labor. First animate the top node, usually the neutral stand. Other motions, such as walk and run, then flow from this one.

If you animate before you get approval and this initial neutral motion is changed, all other motions also need to be changed.

Finally, you need to test all the transitions and bridging motions—in the game engine. Be sure to test early and often to avoid major problems at the end of the production.

Conclusion

Even though the requirements for game animation are much different from those for film, all of the fundamental principles of animation apply. Be sure to be true to your characters, understand them, and try to get the most out of your cycles. Even a short walk cycle can ooze with character in the hands of talented animator.

Index

Colophon

Digital Character Animation 2, Volume II was produced with the help of Microsoft Word, Adobe Photoshop, and QuarkXPress on a variety of systems, including a Macintosh G4. With the exception of pages that were printed for proofreading, all files—both images and text—were transferred via email or ftp and then edited electronically.

All the body text was set in the Bembo family, and all the headings and figure captions were set in the Frutiger family. The Zapf Dingbats and Symbol typefaces were used throughout the book for special symbols and bullets.

This book was printed at R. R. Donnelley in Roanoke, Virginia. Prepress consisted of PostScript computer-to-plate technology (filmless process). The interior pages were printed web press on 60# Mead Web Dull. The cover was printed on 12 pt. C1S at Moore Langen Printing in Terre Haute, Indiana.